Friendship Strips & Scraps

By Edyta Sitar for Laundry Basket Quilts

Landauer Publishing

Acknowledgements

- A very special "Thank You" is extended to the many skilled hands and patient minds that have helped me to make this book possible:

- My loving family and friends who support me in everything I do, especially my mom, children, and husband, Mike.

- Moda Fabrics for the opportunity to design beautiful fabrics that are the starting point for my quilts.

- Julie Lillo, Pam Henrys, and Dan Kolbe for adding the special touch to the machine quilting in these projects.

- Scott and Curtis from Southern Exposure for welcoming me again to their beautiful home and gardens where photography was taken.

- Creative Grids® for providing us with rulers that made the cutting easy and accurate.

- The Landauer Publishing team for their patience, expertise and seemingly endless hours in bringing this book to life. Your hard work, sharing your talents, and always being accommodating will forever be one of my blessings. I thank you for that.

- All the quilters who have enjoyed my designs over the years and exchanged strips with me.

This book was designed, produced, and published by Landauer Corporation
3100 NW 101st Street, Urbandale, IA 50322
800-557-2144; www.landauercorp.com

President/Publisher: Jeramy Lanigan Landauer
Vice President of Sales & Operations: Kitty Jacobson
Managing Editor: Jeri Simon
Art Director: Laurel Albright
Technical Editor: Rhonda Matus
Photography: Sue Voegtlin

Library of Congress Control Number: 2010932628
ISBN 13: 978-1-935726-01-2

This book is printed on acid-free paper.
Printed in China
10 9 8 7 6 5 4 3 2 1

Contents

Projects

Strip Exchange

Let's get together and enjoy each other's company as we exchange fabric through strips. Whether through shops, guilds, retreats, or small groups, fabric exchanges with quilting friends are always special. Get a group of quilting friends together—it doesn't matter how small or big the group is, but remember, more people equal more variety in fabric. With a larger group you can anticipate some unexpected fabric pieces that will add fun and pop to your strip panel.

STRIP EXCHANGE WITH FRIENDS

Decide on Color—As a group decide if strips should be in shades of coordinating colors or if anything goes. You can also base your color choice around a theme or holiday. Exchange strips in a variety of pinks and reds to celebrate Valentine's Day. You may wish to commemorate the Fourth of July with red, white, and blue strips. It's the perfect exchange for cleaning out your fabric stash and enjoying some of your friends fabric choices.

Decide on Strip Size—The strips can be cut in a variety of 1" to 2-1/2" widths. They should always be cut selvage to selvage. Precut fabric strips, such as Jelly Rolls™ and Honey Buns™, can also be used.

Have an Exchange—Gather a group of friends and their friends (remember the more the merrier) and get ready to exchange strips. Say hello to the friends you know and introduce yourself to those you are meeting for the first time. Offer to trade a fabric strip with them or if you really like their fabric offer them a two for one deal—two of your strips for one of theirs. Pretend you are back in grade school trading baseball cards or friendship bracelets. Anything goes!

Equal Numbers—The number of strips each quilter receives should equal the number they have given away, unless they went for the two-for-one deal. Each quilter can keep track of what she gives and receives.

Choose a Project and Begin—Select a project and start sewing. Be sure to get back together with your quilting friends so everyone can show off their newest strip creation. Many projects in the book begin with a strip panel. Since the panel is made up of strips of all sizes it hides any imperfections within the strips. The strip panel technique can be found on pages 10-11.

I love to work with strip panels. It offers a relaxing and rewarding sewing experience. I hope you enjoy this technique as much as I do.

Edyta Sitar

About the Author...

Edyta Sitar is proud to carry on a family tradition that fabrics and threads have seamlessly stitched together through the generations.

Her true love for quilting and her quilter's spirit shines through in her classes, workshops, and presentations. She travels all over sharing her passion, connecting to and inspiring quilters of all levels by sharing personal and stimulating stories about the quilts she makes.

Quilting has opened a door to another world for Edyta, one in which she can express herself, create beautiful designs, and release her artistic passion. The combination of inspiration from nature, a love for fabric, a keen eye for color, and her family teachings blended into the recipe for developing a flourishing talent for designing quilts, fabrics, and quilting patterns.

"My children and my husband are my greatest motivation, providing the basis that you can accomplish anything you want if you just set your mind to it. Being able to do what I love and share this love with others is the greatest feeling and reward I could imagine! This is the Cinderella dream for me."

As the owner and co-founder of Laundry Basket Quilts, her work has been published in magazines world-wide and her quilts have received numerous awards.

Edyta resides in Marshall, Michigan with her husband and children where she enjoys creating beautiful patterns for Laundry Basket Quilts and designing splendid fabrics for MODA.

Strip Panels

Strip panels are easy to make and a great way to use all those leftover strips and fabric scraps. Share strips with friends to achieve a beautiful one-of-a-kind color scheme.

Straighten fabric edges before cutting your strips. Cut fabric strips between 1" and 2-1/2" wide. Vary the width of the strips if desired. Always cut from selvage to selvage. Due to the differences in fabric width, the length of your strips will be between 40" and 44".

Supplies—Fabric or fabric scraps, cotton thread (I prefer Aurifil™ 2370 for color; it blends beautifully with any fabric), acrylic ruler, rotary cutter, and cutting mat.

Even when choosing fabric scraps remember to follow my Rule of Five. Pick a big print, medium print, small print, stripe, and polka dot. This will give your project a beautiful look and a nice texture.

Layer two strips, right sides together and sew along one long edge, using a 1/4" seam allowance. Press the seams in one direction.

Here's a Tip

Take advantage of wonderful precut fabrics such as Jelly Rolls™ and Honey Buns™ from Moda. You will get a variety of colors in ready to sew precut strips. Fat quarter bundles also work well for scrappy projects.

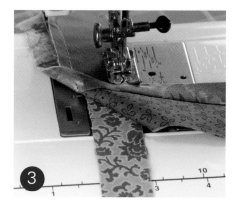

Place a third strip on the strip panel aligning the long edges. Begin sewing the third strip at the opposite end where you joined the first two strips. Press seams in same direction as first two strips. **You may wish to flip the fabric so the strip panel is laying on top when sewing. This will keep the strip panel from 'waving'.**

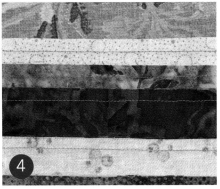

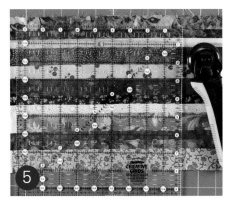

Here's a Tip

If you have strips that are uneven or too short for the strip panel but are the same width, sew them together until they equal 40"-44" in length. Use a matching or contrasting fabric strip to add a scrappy look to your finished project.

4 Continue adding strips to the strip panel, aligning long edges and alternating the direction they are sewn together. Press all seams in the same direction.

5 The final strip panel should be no larger than 18" x approximately 40"-44" (fabric length will vary). A strip panel this size is easy to sew and will accommodate any of the shapes and templates you need to cut. If you have chosen a project, the strip panel should be approximately 1" larger than your block or template size. With your ruler cut out the size of blocks needed for your project.

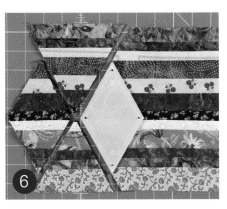

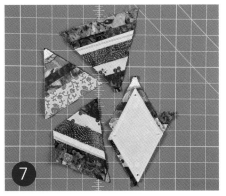

6 If using a template, lay the chosen template over the strip panel. Be sure the tip of the template is not laying on a seam line. Cut around the template to create the shape needed for your project.

7 Use every bit of the strip panel by taking the triangles left over from cutting the diamonds and piecing them, right sides together. Press open and place the diamond template on top. Cut around the template to create another diamond.

Full-size templates for each project may be found in the book. Acrylic templates, as well as Appliqué Silhouettes sheets, may be purchased at **www.laundrybasketquilts.com**.

Fusible Appliqué

This style of appliqué has become my personal favorite. With a little patience and the right materials you can achieve excellent results in a short period of time. I also find it to be a relaxing and enjoyable technique.

Supplies

Light fusible webbing, pressing sheet, sharp scissors, traced block layout, reversed appliqué pieces, pencil, cotton thread for sewing the **buttonhole stitch** and for the bobbin (I prefer Aurifil™ 2370 in the bobbin), nylon invisible thread for sewing the **zigzag stitch**, embroidery 75/11 needle for machine, background fabric, and desired appliqué fabric

Note: Appliqué Silhouettes from Laundry Basket Quilts will allow you to draw many of the appliqué patterns quickly and easily. They are not necessary to complete any of the projects in this book but are a useful tool.

To prepare the appliqués, place the fusible webbing, paper side up on the reversed appliqué shapes. Trace each appliqué shape, including any dashed lines, onto the fusible webbing. Mark each shape with its corresponding letter to help you place the pieces correctly on the layout. **Note:** All shapes in the book are conveniently reversed for this technique. If using Appliqué Silhouettes for tracing be sure to match them to the images in the book.

Cut out the appliqué shapes from the fusible webbing leaving at least ¹⁄₈" of fusible webbing around the outside of each shape. You may cut the fusible webbing from the center of the larger pieces, if you wish.

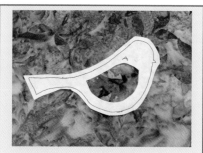

Here's a Tip

To remove the fusible webbing from the center of larger template shapes, such as the bird, cut into the center of the webbing with a sharp scissors. Cut out the center leaving approximately ¹⁄₄" inside the traced line.

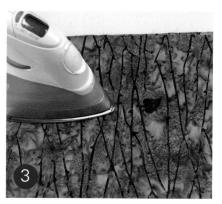

Press your fabrics before fusing to be sure there are no wrinkles or creases.

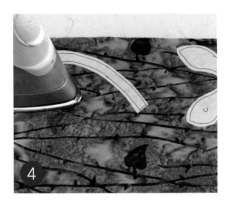

Fuse each appliqué shape by pressing it to the **wrong side** of the desired color fabric following manufacturer's directions on fusible webbing. **Note:** Do not overheat fusible webbing.

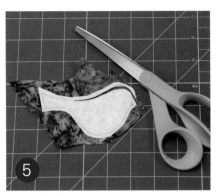

Cut the appliqué shapes out **exactly** on the traced line. Achieve nice smooth edges by using the back blades of a sharp scissors and making long cuts.

Place the traced layout guide under the pressing sheet on an ironing board. Proceed to prepare the appliqué pieces to place on the background.

Peel the fusible webbing paper from each shape.
Note: If you crease the edge of the paper it will peel off easier.

After all the paper is peeled off, place each fabric appliquéd shape on top of the pressing sheet, following the layout underneath as a placement guide.
Note: Remember the dashed lines indicate where the fabric shapes overlap each other.

Press the appliqué shapes together *only* where the fabric appliqués overlap. Press gently to secure these pieces together. Make sure all your pieces stay on the layout and use it as your guide.

Fusible Appliqué continued

10

Peel the group of appliqué shapes from the pressing sheet and place where desired on your block. Press in place.

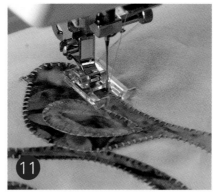

11

Stitch around all edges of the appliqués with a buttonhole stitch. I love using my favorite Aurifil™ threads to give extra detail to the edges of my appliqués. I match the top thread color to the color of the appliqué fabric and use Aurifil™ 2370 in the bobbin.
If desired use a zigzag stitch to finish the edge of your appliqué.

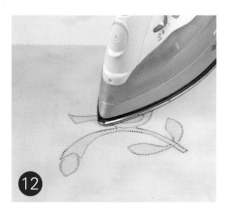

12

When you have completed stitching the shapes to the fabric, gently press from the back. This will heal any holes left by the needle. Be careful that the iron is not too hot. You don't want to overpress and melt the fusible web through the fabric.

13

The appliquéd block is now ready to add to your project.
Note: Fusible appliqué is always easier when done in sections, such as blocks or borders, and then sewn to the quilt top. You can add more appliqué pieces if desired.

Stitch Style

Buttonhole stitch around the edge of the appliqué.
Note: Actual size of stitch is shown.

Top thread - cotton 50 wt.
Bobbin thread - cotton to match background (I use Aurifil™ 2370)
Needle - Embroidery 75/11
Stitch - Buttonhole
Tension - Slightly lower so no bobbin thread shows on top of appliqué

Here's a Tip

To lock your stitches when sewing, overlap the beginning and ending stitches. Gently pull all the thread to the back once the block is completed.

Stitch Style

Zigzag stitch around the edge of the appliqué.
Note: Actual size of stitch is shown.

Top thread - nylon invisible
Bobbin thread - cotton to match background (I use Aurifil™ 2370)
Needle - Embroidery 75/11
Stitch - Zigzag
Tension - Varies from 0-1 on top depending on sewing machine

Materials

- Variety of medium-to-dark 1-1/4"-wide print and batik strips (approximately 56 strips)
- 2-1/2 yards of light batik for foundation blocks, blocks, and inner border
- 1/2 yard total assorted dark prints and batiks for blocks
- 1/2 yard total assorted red prints and batiks for inner border
- 5/8 yard brown batik for outer border
- 1/2 yard red print for binding
- 12—3" x 6" rectangles of assorted medium-to-dark prints and batiks for door appliqués
- 12—5" squares of assorted light-to-medium prints and batiks for window appliqués
- 4—4" squares of assorted red prints and batiks for apple appliqués
- Assorted red print and batik scraps for cherry appliqués
- 1/2 yard total assorted green prints and batiks for leaf appliqués
- 3/4 yard total assorted brown prints and batiks for branch and stem appliqués
- 6" square blue batik for bird body appliqués
- 2" x 6" rectangle of green print for bird wing appliqués
- 4—4" x 5" rectangles of assorted gold and green batiks for pear appliqués
- 3-7/8 yards backing fabric
- 68" square batting

Finished block: 10" square
Finished quilt: 61-1/2" x 61-1/2"

Quantities are for 40/44"-wide, 100% cotton fabrics. Measurements include 1/4" seam allowances. Sew with right sides together unless otherwise stated.

NOTE: Refer to Strip Panels on page 10 to sew together the medium-to-dark 1-1/4"-wide print and batik strips to form a strip panel approximately 8-1/2" tall. Press seams in one direction. Make approximately 3 strip panels to cut a total of 12—10-1/2" x 7-1/2" rectangles for the house fronts.

Cut the Fabrics:

From strip panels, cut:
12—10-1/2" x 7-1/2" rectangles

From light batik, cut:
13—13"-square appliqué foundation blocks
10—6-1/4" squares, cutting each diagonally in an X for a total of 40 inner border triangles
24—3-1/2" squares
From assorted dark prints and batiks, cut:
12—10-1/2" x 3-1/2" roof rectangles
From assorted red prints and batiks, cut:
11—6-1/4" squares, cutting each diagonally in an X for a total of 44 inner border triangles
From brown batik, cut:
6—3-1/2" x 42" outer border strips
From red print, cut:
6—2-1/2" x 42" binding strips
From backing, cut:
2—34-1/2" x 68" rectangles

Cut the Appliqués

The following instructions are for cutting the appliqués for the 12 farmhouse blocks and the 13 appliquéd blocks. Trace the appliqué patterns on page 21. Use the appliqué method of your choice to prepare appliqué pieces.

From medium-to-dark prints and batiks, cut:

12—2" x 5-1/2" door appliqués

From light-to-medium prints and batiks, cut:

24—2"-square window appliqués, cutting two matching windows for 10 blocks and two different windows for the remaining two blocks

From red prints and batiks, cut:

4 of pattern A (apple)

5 of pattern B (cherry)

4 of pattern L (cherry)

From green prints and batiks, cut:

25 of pattern C (leaf)

21 of pattern C reversed (leaf)

From brown prints and batiks, cut:

13 of pattern D (branch)

8 of pattern E (branch)

4 of pattern F (apple stem)

10 of pattern G (cherry stem)

4 of pattern H (pear stem)

From blue batik, cut:

3 of pattern I (bird body)

From green print, cut:

3 of pattern J (bird wing)

From gold and green batiks, cut:

4 of pattern K (pear)

Assemble and Appliqué the Farmhouse Blocks

1. Draw a diagonal line across the wrong side of two light batik 3-1/2" squares.

2. Place light batik 3-1/2" squares on the top corners of a dark print or batik 10-1/2" x 3-1/2" rectangle, right sides together, as shown for the roof section. Sew on the drawn lines. Trim seams to 1/4" and press seams toward the triangles.

   Note: Reserve the trimmed triangles to use in the border for the Family Estate Wallhanging on page 96.

3. Sew the roof section to the 10-1/2" x 7-1/2" strip panel rectangle. Press seams toward roof section.

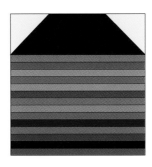

4. Position a door and two window appliqué pieces on the house front, aligning the bottom edges of the door and the strip panel rectangle. Appliqué in place using your favorite method.

5. Repeat Steps 1-4 to make a total of 12 farmhouse blocks.

Assemble the Appliqué Blocks

1. Position a D appliqué on each light batik 13" foundation block. Align the bottom edges of D and the foundation block so the end of D will be included later in the bottom seam.

2. Referring to the photograph on page 22 as a guide, arrange one set of appliqué pieces around each D appliqué. Note that some pieces (E and those connected to E) extend beyond a single block; set these aside until the quilt center is assembled. Work only with the pieces connected to D at this time. For example, use one D, two Cs, one H, and one K for the first

appliqué block in the second row; the remaining appliqué shapes on this block will be added later.

3. Appliqué the shapes in place using your favorite method. Press appliquéd blocks from the back. Center and trim each to a 10-1/2" square.

Assemble the Quilt Center

1. Referring to Quilt Center Assembly Diagram, lay out 12 farmhouse blocks and 13 appliquéd blocks in five horizontal rows.

2. Sew together the blocks in each row. Press seams toward the appliquéd blocks.

3. Join rows. Press seams in one direction.

4. Referring to the photograph on page 22 as a guide, position the set aside appliqué pieces on the quilt top and appliqué the shapes in place using your favorite method.

Quilt Center Assembly Diagram

Add the Borders

1. Sew together 9 light batik triangles and 9 red print or batik triangles in pairs. Offset the triangles approximately 1/4" as shown. Press open and trim the tips if desired.

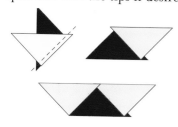

2. Join the pairs together to make an inner border. Sew a light batik triangle to the end of the strip. Repeat to make four inner border strips.

Make 4

3. Referring to Quilt Top Assembly Diagram, sew an inner border strip to each edge of the quilt center.

4. Sew the remaining red print or batik triangles together in pairs as shown. Add these to the corners of the quilt top to complete the inner border.

5. Piece the 3-1/2" x 42" outer border strips to make the following: 2–3-1/2" x 55-1/2" for top and bottom and 2–3-1/2" x 61-1/2" for sides.

6. Sew top and bottom outer border strips to the quilt center. Press seams toward border. Add the side outer border strips to the quilt center. Press seams toward border.

Quilt Top Assembly Diagram

Complete the Quilt

1. Sew together the 34-1/2" x 68" backing rectangles along one long edge, using a 1/2" seam allowance. Press the seam allowance open.

2. Layer quilt top, batting, and pieced backing.

3. Quilt as desired. Neutral thread was used to stitch closely around each appliqué shape and along the edges of the farmhouse roof and front. The farmhouse fronts are filled with stippling and the roofs are filled with a variety of patterns. The background and borders are filled with an allover swirl pattern.

4. Bind with red print binding strips.

Farmhouse Quilt

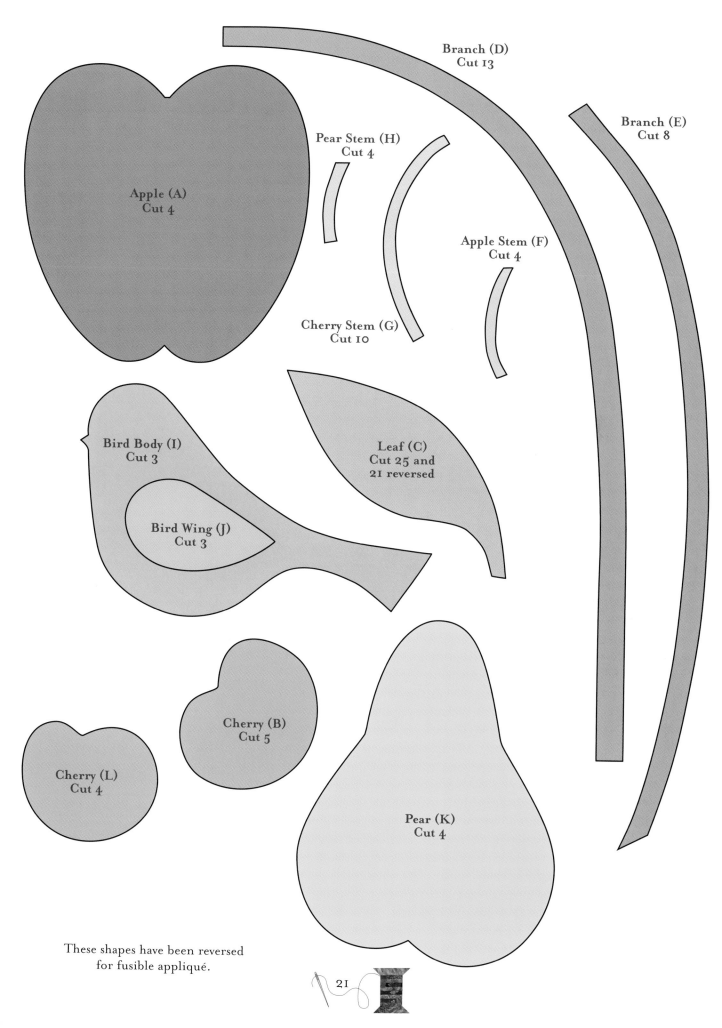

Branch (D)
Cut 13

Branch (E)
Cut 8

Pear Stem (H)
Cut 4

Apple (A)
Cut 4

Apple Stem (F)
Cut 4

Cherry Stem (G)
Cut 10

Leaf (C)
Cut 25 and
21 reversed

Bird Body (I)
Cut 3

Bird Wing (J)
Cut 3

Cherry (B)
Cut 5

Cherry (L)
Cut 4

Pear (K)
Cut 4

These shapes have been reversed
for fusible appliqué.

Farmhouse Quilt

Designed and pieced by Edyta Sitar for Laundry Basket Quilts

Stacked Scraps Quilt

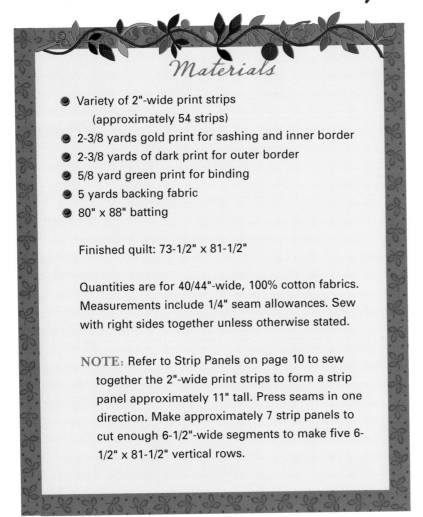

Materials

- Variety of 2"-wide print strips
  (approximately 54 strips)
- 2-3/8 yards gold print for sashing and inner border
- 2-3/8 yards of dark print for outer border
- 5/8 yard green print for binding
- 5 yards backing fabric
- 80" x 88" batting

Finished quilt: 73-1/2" x 81-1/2"

Quantities are for 40/44"-wide, 100% cotton fabrics. Measurements include 1/4" seam allowances. Sew with right sides together unless otherwise stated.

NOTE: Refer to Strip Panels on page 10 to sew together the 2"-wide print strips to form a strip panel approximately 11" tall. Press seams in one direction. Make approximately 7 strip panels to cut enough 6-1/2"-wide segments to make five 6-1/2" x 81-1/2" vertical rows.

Cut the Fabrics

From strip panels, cut:
6-1/2"-wide segments, no more
    than 11"-tall, to make five
    6-1/2" x 81-1/2" pieced
    vertical rows

From gold print, cut:
4—6-1/2" x 81-1/2" sashing strips
2—2-1/2" x 81-1/2" inner
    border strips

From dark print, cut:
2—8" x 81-1/2" outer border strips

From green print, cut:
8—2-1/2" x 42" binding strips

From backing, cut:
2—40-1/2" x 88" rectangles

Assemble the Quilt Center

1. Lay out enough 6-1/2"-wide segments to create an 81-1/2" vertical row. Sew the segments together; press seams in one direction. Repeat to make a total of five 6-1/2" x 81-1/2" rows.

Make 5

2. Measure to check the length of the pieced rows. If necessary, make minor adjustments to some seams to adjust the length so all rows measure 81-1/2".

Stacked Scraps Quilt

3. Referring to Quilt Center Assembly Diagram, sew the gold print 6-1/2"-wide sashing strips to the long edges of the rows to complete the quilt center. Press seams toward sashing strips.

Add the Borders

1. Sew the gold print 2-1/2"-wide inner border strips to the left and right edges of the quilt center. Press seams toward border.

2. Add the dark print 8"-wide outer border strips to the left and right edges of the quilt center. Press seams toward outer border.

Complete the Quilt

1. Sew together the 40-1/2" x 88" backing rectangles along one long edge, using a 1/2" seam allowance. Press the seam allowance open.

2. Layer quilt top, batting, and pieced backing.

3. Quilt as desired. A variegated thread was used to stitch an allover whimsical design.

4. Bind with green print binding strips.

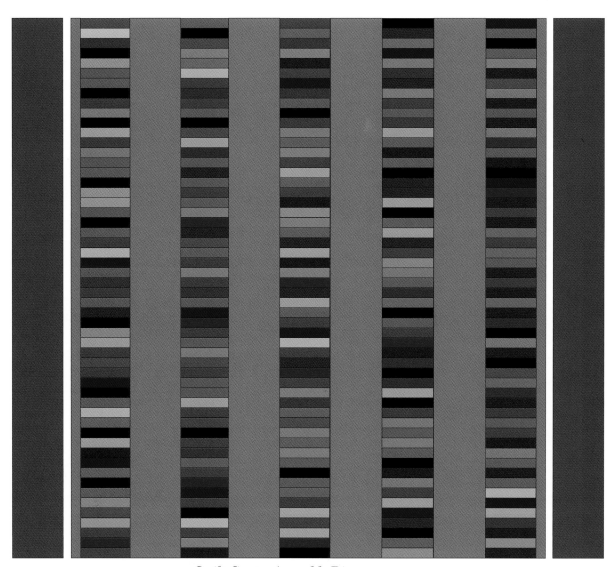

Quilt Center Assembly Diagram

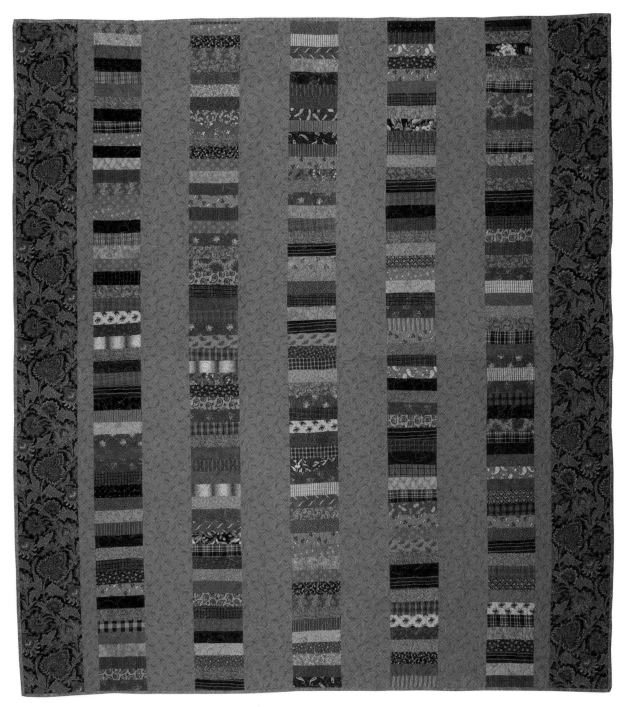

Stacked Scraps Quilt
Designed and pieced by Edyta Sitar for Laundry Basket Quilts

Shutters Quilt

Materials

- Assorted yellow and green 1-1/4"-wide print and batik strips for 4-patch block center (4 yellow strips and 4 green strips)
- Variety of dark 1-1/4"-wide print and batik strips (approximately 100 strips)
- Variety of light 1-1/4"-wide print and batik strips (approximately 110 strips)
- 5/8 yard dark batik for binding
- 5 yards backing fabric
- 82" x 89" batting

Finished block: 7-1/2" square
Finished quilt: 75-1/2" x 83"

Quantities are for 40/44"-wide, 100% cotton fabrics. Measurements include 1/4" seam allowances. Sew with right sides together unless otherwise stated.

Cut the Fabrics

From assorted dark 1-1/4"-wide print and batik strips, cut:

110 — 1-1/4" x 2" A logs
110 — 1-1/4" x 3-1/2" B logs
110 — 1-1/4" x 3-1/2" C logs
110 — 1-1/4" x 5" D logs
110 — 1-1/4" x 5" E logs
110 — 1-1/4" x 6-1/2" F logs
110 — 1-1/4" x 6-1/2" G logs
110 — 1-1/4" x 8" H logs

From assorted light 1-1/4"-wide print and batik strips, cut:

110 — 1-1/4" x 2" A logs
110 — 1-1/4" x 3-1/2" B logs
110 — 1-1/4" x 3-1/2" C logs
110 — 1-1/4" x 5" D logs
110 — 1-1/4" x 5" E logs
110 — 1-1/4" x 6-1/2" F logs
110 — 1-1/4" x 6-1/2" G logs
110 — 1-1/4" x 8" H logs

From dark batik, cut:

8 — 2-1/2" x 42" binding strips

From backing, cut:

2 — 41-1/2" x 89" rectangles

Make the Four-Patch Block Centers

1. Sew 1-1/4"-wide green and yellow strips, right sides together, along one long edge to make strip sets. Press seams toward dark strip.

2. Cut the strip sets into 220 — 1-1/4"-wide segments.

1-1/4"

3. Sew together segments in pairs as shown to make 110 four-patch block centers. Press seams in one direction.

Make 110

Assemble the Courthouse Steps Blocks

1. Sew dark print or batik 1-1/4" x 2" A logs to opposite edges of a four-patch block center. Press seams away from center.

2. Sew light print or batik 1-1/4" x 3-1/2" B logs to the remaining edges of the four-patch center. Press seams away from center.

3. Continue adding the logs in this manner around the four-patch center. Join logs in alphabetical order, using a pattern of two dark logs followed by two light logs as shown. Press seams away from the center after each log addition.

4. Repeat Steps 1-3 to make a total of 55 light courthouse steps blocks.

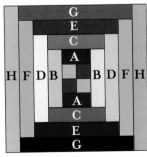

Make 55 Light Blocks

Shutters Quilt

5. Repeat Steps 1–3 to make a total of 55 dark courthouse steps blocks, reversing the pattern to two light logs followed by two dark logs as shown.

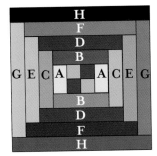

Make 55 Dark Blocks

Assemble the Quilt Top

1. Referring to Quilt Top Assembly Diagram, lay out 55 light courthouse steps blocks and 55 dark courthouse steps blocks in eleven horizontal rows, alternating dark and light blocks as shown.
2. Sew together blocks in each row. Press seams in one direction, alternating the direction from row to row.
3. Join rows. Press seams in one direction.

Complete the Quilt

1. Sew together the 41-1/2" x 89" backing rectangles along one long edge, using a 1/2" seam allowance. Press the seam allowance open.
2. Layer quilt top, batting, and pieced backing.
3. Quilt as desired. The quilt was stitched using neutral thread for an allover stippling pattern.
4. Bind with dark batik binding strips.

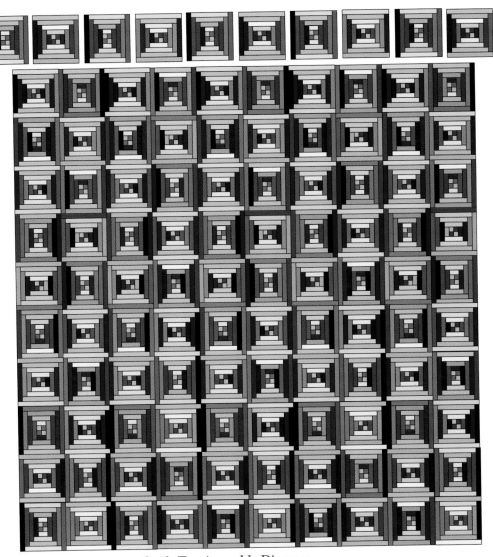

Quilt Top Assembly Diagram

Shutters Quilt

Designed and pieced by Edyta Sitar for Laundry Basket Quilts

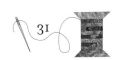

Dollhouse Table Topper

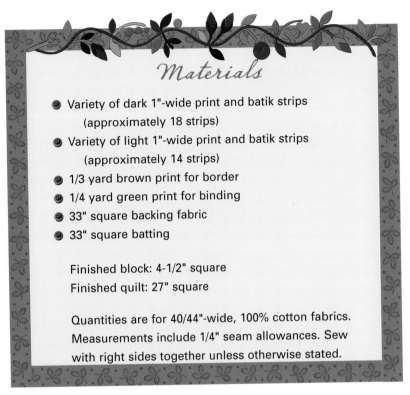

Materials

- Variety of dark 1"-wide print and batik strips (approximately 18 strips)
- Variety of light 1"-wide print and batik strips (approximately 14 strips)
- 1/3 yard brown print for border
- 1/4 yard green print for binding
- 33" square backing fabric
- 33" square batting

Finished block: 4-1/2" square
Finished quilt: 27" square

Quantities are for 40/44"-wide, 100% cotton fabrics. Measurements include 1/4" seam allowances. Sew with right sides together unless otherwise stated.

3. Continue adding the logs in a clockwise direction around the center square. Join logs in alphabetical order, using a pattern of two light logs followed by two dark logs as shown. Press seams away from the center after each log addition.

4. Repeat Steps 1-3 to make a total of twenty-five log cabin blocks.

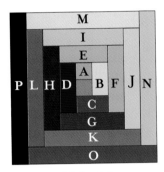

Make 25

Cut the Fabrics

From assorted dark 1"-wide print and batik strips, cut:

25 – 1" center squares
25 – 1" x 1-1/2" C logs
25 – 1" x 2" D logs
25 – 1" x 2-1/2" G logs
25 – 1" x 3" H logs
25 – 1" x 3-1/2" K logs
25 – 1" x 4" L logs
25 – 1" x 4-1/2" O logs
25 – 1" x 5" P logs

From assorted light 1"-wide print and batik strips, cut:

25 – 1" square A logs
25 – 1" x 1-1/2" B logs
25 – 1" x 2" E logs
25 – 1" x 2-1/2" F logs
25 – 1" x 3" I logs
25 – 1" x 3-1/2" J logs
25 – 1" x 4" M logs
25 – 1" x 4-1/2" N logs

From brown print, cut:

2 – 2-1/2" x 23" border strips
2 – 2-1/2" x 27" border strips

From medium print, cut:

3 – 2-1/2" x 42" binding strips

Assemble the Log Cabin Blocks

1. Sew a light print or batik 1" square A log to a dark print or batik 1" center square. Press seam away from center square.

2. Sew a light print or batik 1" x 1-1/2" B log to the center square/A log from Step 1. Press seam toward B.

Dollhouse Table Topper

Assemble the Table Topper Center

1. Referring to Table Topper Center Assembly Diagram, lay out twenty-five log cabin blocks in five horizontal rows as shown.
2. Sew together blocks in each row. Press seams in one direction, alternating the direction from row to row.
3. Join rows. Press seams in one direction.

Add the Border

1. Referring to the Table Topper Assembly Diagram, sew 2-1/2" x 23" border strips to opposite edges of the table topper center. Press seams toward border.
2. Add 2-1/2" x 27" border strips to remaining edges. Press seams toward the border.

Complete the Table Topper

1. Layer table topper top, batting, and backing.
2. Quilt as desired. The quilt was stitched using a feather pattern over the entire quilt top.
3. Bind with green print binding strips.

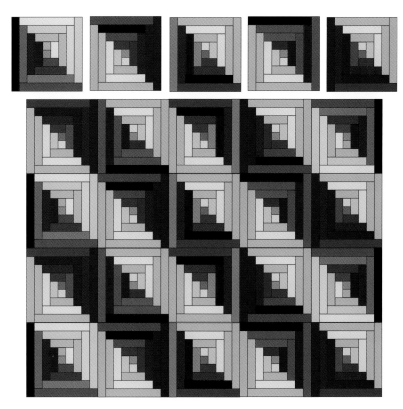

Table Topper Center Assembly Diagram

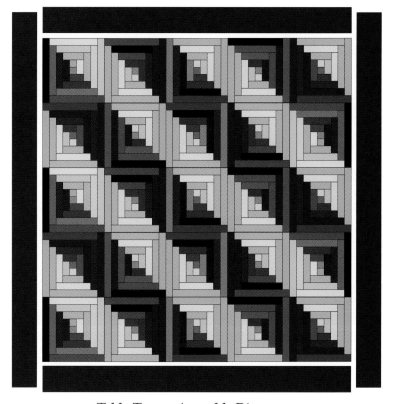

Table Topper Assembly Diagram

Dollhouse Table Topper
Designed and pieced by Edyta Sitar for Laundry Basket Quilts

Seven Sisters Quilt

Materials

- Variety of dark 1"-wide print and batik strips (approximately 84 strips)
- Variety of light 1"-wide print and batik strips (approximately 94 strips)
- 1/3 yard light print for inner border
- 3/4 yard dark batik for outer border
- 5/8 yard red print for binding
- 4 yards backing fabric
- 70" square batting

Finished block: 4-1/2" square
Finished quilt: 63-1/2" square

Quantities are for 40/44"-wide, 100% cotton fabrics. Measurements include 1/4" seam allowances. Sew with right sides together unless otherwise stated.

Cut the Fabrics

NOTE: Use dark pink-to-red 1" center squares for the 20 light log cabin blocks.

From assorted dark 1"-wide print and batik strips, cut:

144 – 1" center squares (I selected pinks and reds for my centers)
124 – 1" x 1-1/2" C logs
124 – 1" x 2" D logs
124 – 1" x 2-1/2" G logs
124 – 1" x 3" H logs
124 – 1" x 3-1/2" K logs
124 – 1" x 4" L logs
124 – 1" x 4-1/2" O logs
124 – 1" x 5" P logs

From assorted light 1"-wide print and batik strips, cut:

144 – 1" square A logs
164 – 1" x 1-1/2" B/C logs
164 – 1" x 2" D/E logs
164 – 1" x 2-1/2" F/G logs
164 – 1" x 3" H/I logs
164 – 1" x 3-1/2" J/K logs
164 – 1" x 4" L/M logs
164 – 1" x 4-1/2" N/O logs
20 – 1" x 5" P logs

From light print, cut:

6 – 1-1/2" x 42" inner border strips

From dark batik, cut:

6 – 4" x 42" outer border strips

From red print, cut:

7 – 2-1/2" x 42" binding strips

From backing, cut:

2 – 35-1/2" x 70" rectangles

Assemble the Dark/Light Log Cabin Blocks

1. Sew a light print or batik 1" square A log to a dark print or batik 1" center square. Press seam away from center square.

2. Sew a light print or batik 1" x 1-1/2" B log to the center square/A log from Step 1. Press seam toward B.

3. Continue adding the logs in a clockwise direction around the center square. Join logs in alphabetical order, using a pattern of two light logs followed by two dark logs as shown. Press seams away from the center after each log addition.

4. Repeat Steps 1–3 to make a total of 124 dark/light log cabin blocks.

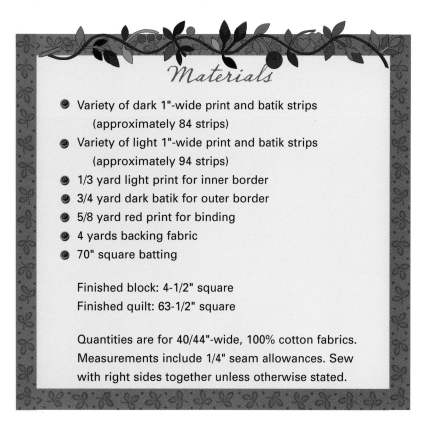

Make 124 Dark/Light Blocks

Assemble the Light Log Cabin Blocks

1. Sew a light print or batik 1" square A log to a dark pink-to-red 1" center square. Press seam away from center square.

2. Sew a light print or batik 1" x 1-1/2" B log to the center square/A log from Step 1. Press seam toward B.

3. Continue adding the logs in a clockwise direction around the center square. Join logs in alphabetical order, using only light logs as shown. Press seams away from the center after each log addition.

4. Repeat Steps 1–3 to make a total of 20 light log cabin blocks.

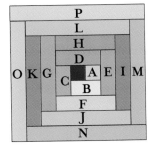

Make 20 Light Blocks

Assemble the Quilt Center

1. Referring to Quilt Center Assembly Diagram, lay out 124 dark/light log cabin blocks and 20 light log cabin blocks in twelve horizontal rows as shown.

2. Sew together blocks in each row. Press seams in one direction, alternating the direction from row to row.

3. Join rows. Press seams in one direction.

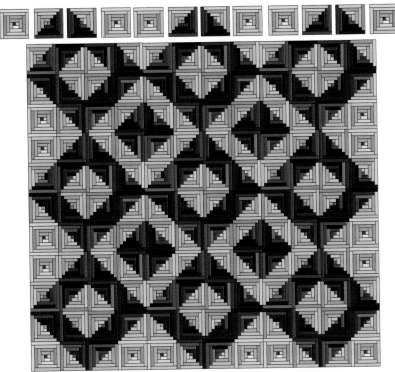

Quilt Center Assembly Diagram

Add the Borders

1. Piece the 1-1/2" x 42" inner border strips to make the following: 2 – 1-1/2" x 54-1/2" for top and bottom and 2 – 1-1/2" x 56-1/2" for sides.

2. Referring to the Quilt Top Assembly Diagram, sew the top and bottom inner border strips to the quilt center. Press seams toward border. Sew the side inner border strips to the quilt center. Press seams toward border.

3. Piece the 4" x 42" outer border strips to make the following: 2 – 4" x 56-1/2" for top and bottom and 2 – 4" x 63-1/2" for sides.

4. Sew the top and bottom outer border strips to the quilt center. Press seams toward border. Sew the side outer border strips to the quilt center. Press seams toward border.

Complete the Quilt

1. Sew together the 35-1/2" x 70" backing rectangles along one long edge, using a 1/2" seam allowance. Press the seam allowance open.

2. Layer quilt top, batting, and pieced backing.

3. Quilt as desired. The quilt was stitched using neutral thread for an allover swirl pattern.

4. Bind with red print binding strips.

Quilt Top Assembly Diagram

Quilt Top Diagram

Seven Sisters Quilt
Designed and pieced by Edyta Sitar for Laundry Basket Quilts

Shimmering Birches Quilt

Materials

- Variety of dark 1-1/4"-wide print and batik strips for nine-patch units (approximately 27 strips)
- Variety of light 1-1/4"-wide print and batik strips for nine-patch units (approximately 22 strips)
- Assorted dark print and batik scraps for block centers (1/8 yard)
- 5/8 yard cream print for blocks
- 1 yard tan print for sashing
- 5/8 yard medium batik for border
- 1/2 yard dark print for binding
- 3-3/8 yards backing fabric
- 60" square batting

Finished block: 6" square
Finished quilt: 53-3/4" square

Quantities are for 40/44"-wide, 100% cotton fabrics. Measurements include 1/4" seam allowances. Sew with right sides together unless otherwise stated.

Cut the Fabrics

From assorted dark print and batik scraps, cut:

36 — 2" center squares

From cream print, cut:

144 — 2" x 2-3/4" rectangles

From tan print, cut:

60 — 2-3/4" x 6-1/2" sashing strips

From medium batik, cut:

5 — 3-1/2" x 42" border strips

From dark print, cut:

6 — 2-1/2" x 42" binding strips

From backing, cut:

2 — 30-1/2" x 60" rectangles

Make the Nine-Patch Units

1. Sew together two dark 1-1/4"-wide print or batik strips and one light 1-1/4"-wide print or batik strip to make a dark/light/dark strip set as shown. Cut the strip set into 1-1/4"-wide segments. Make enough dark/light/dark strip sets to cut 338 — 1-1/4"-wide segments.

1-1/4"

2. Sew together two light 1-1/4"-wide print or batik strips and one dark 1-1/4"-wide print or batik strip to make a light/dark/light strip set as shown. Cut the strip set into 1-1/4"-wide segments. Make enough light/dark/light strip sets to cut 169 — 1-1/4"-wide segments.

1-1/4"

3. Sew together two dark/light/dark segments and one light/dark/light segment to make a nine-patch unit as shown. Press seams in one direction. Repeat to make a total of 169 nine-patch units.

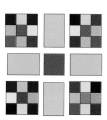

Make 169

Assemble the Blocks

1. Lay out four nine-patch units, four cream print 2" x 2-3/4" rectangles, and one dark print or batik 2" center square as shown.

2. Sew the pieces together in rows. Press the seams toward the rectangles.
3. Sew the rows together to complete one block.
4. Repeat Steps 1-3 to make a total of 36 blocks.

Make 36

Shimmering Birches Quilt

Assemble the Quilt Center

1. Referring to Quilt Center Assembly Diagram, lay out 36 blocks, the 25 remaining nine-patch units, and 60 tan print 2-3/4" x 6-1/2" sashing strips as shown.

2. Sew the pieces together in rows. Press seams toward sashing strips.

3. Join the rows to make the quilt center. Press seams in one direction.

Add the Border

1. Piece the medium batik 3-1/2" x 42" border strips to make the following: 2 − 3-1/2" x 47-3/4" for top and bottom and 2 − 3-1/2" x 53-3/4" for sides.

2. Referring to Quilt Top Assembly Diagram, sew the top and bottom border strips to the quilt center. Press seams toward border. Sew the side border strips to the quilt center. Press seams toward border.

Complete the Quilt

1. Sew together the 30-1/2" x 60" backing rectangles along one long edge, using a 1/2" seam allowance. Press the seam allowance open.

2. Layer quilt top, batting, and pieced backing.

3. Quilt as desired. The quilt was stitched using a rainbow arch pattern over the entire quilt top.

4. Bind with dark print binding strips.

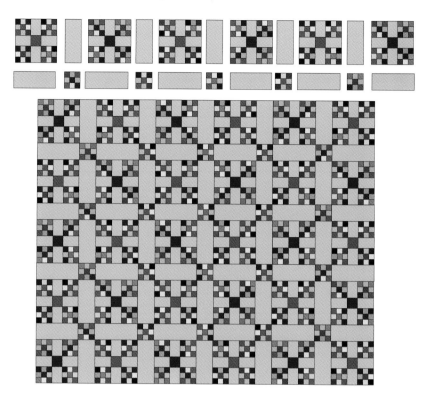

Quilt Center Assembly Diagram

Quilt Top Assembly Diagram

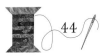

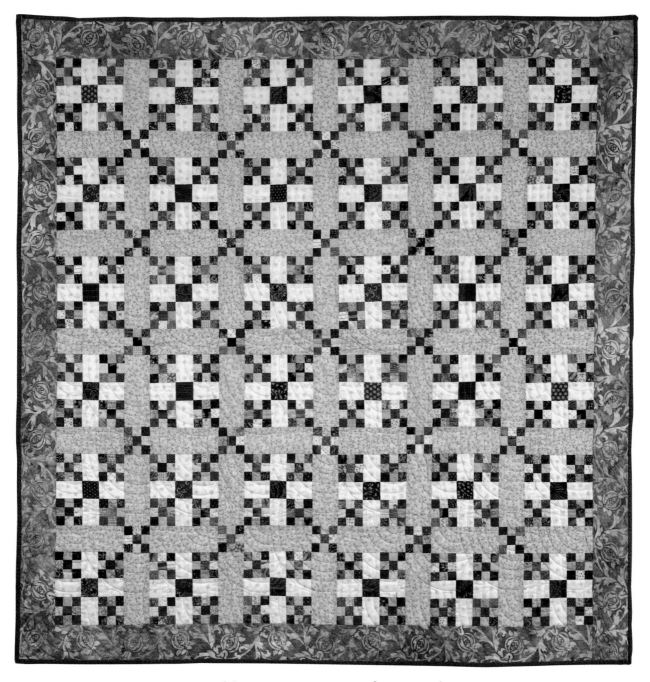

Shimmering Birches Quilt

Designed and pieced by Edyta Sitar for Laundry Basket Quilts

Tumbling Block Table Runner

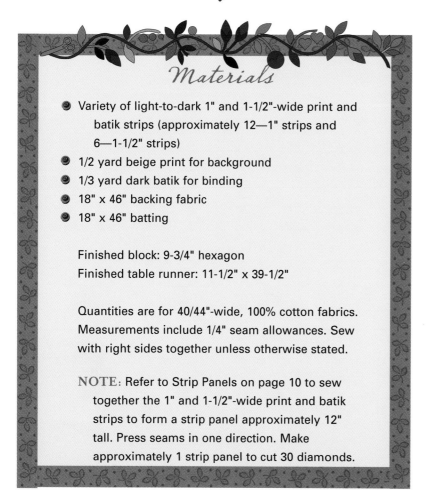

Materials

- Variety of light-to-dark 1" and 1-1/2"-wide print and batik strips (approximately 12—1" strips and 6—1-1/2" strips)
- 1/2 yard beige print for background
- 1/3 yard dark batik for binding
- 18" x 46" backing fabric
- 18" x 46" batting

Finished block: 9-3/4" hexagon
Finished table runner: 11-1/2" x 39-1/2"

Quantities are for 40/44"-wide, 100% cotton fabrics. Measurements include 1/4" seam allowances. Sew with right sides together unless otherwise stated.

NOTE: Refer to Strip Panels on page 10 to sew together the 1" and 1-1/2"-wide print and batik strips to form a strip panel approximately 12" tall. Press seams in one direction. Make approximately 1 strip panel to cut 30 diamonds.

Cut the Fabrics

From strip panels, cut:

30 diamonds using template A on page 48. Position the template so the strips run across the width of each diamond as shown

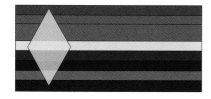

Note: Refer to page 11 to make additional diamonds from the strip panel scraps.

From beige print, cut:

24 diamonds using template A on page 48.

From dark batik, cut:

4 – 2-1/2" x 42" binding strips

Marking the Diamonds

For ease in piecing the Six-Pointed Star blocks, you may find it helpful to mark all the diamonds. Use a ruler and pencil to lightly draw a line or dot to indicate the starting and stopping points for the 1/4" set-in seams.

Assemble the Six-Pointed Star Blocks

1. For one Six-Pointed Star block you will need six strip panel diamonds and six beige print diamonds.

2. Sew together three strip panel diamonds as shown, taking care not to sew into the 1/4" seam allowance. Backstitch to secure seam ends. Press seams in one direction.

3. Sew a beige diamond into the corner between two strip panel diamonds. Sew from the inner corner to the outside edge, backstitching at the inner corner to secure. Pin the adjacent strip panel diamond to the beige diamond. Sew from inner corner to outside edge. Repeat with a second beige diamond at the remaining corner to make a star half. Press seams toward beige diamonds.

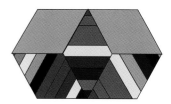

4. Repeat Steps 2 and 3 to make a second star half.

Tumbling Block Table Runner

5. Sew together two star halves without sewing into the 1/4" seam allowance. Sew beige diamonds into remaining corners to make a Six-Pointed Star block. Press seams toward the diamonds.

6. Repeat Steps 1–5 to make a total of four Six-Pointed Star blocks.

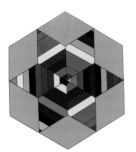

Make 4

Assemble the Table Runner

1. Sew the blocks together as shown, taking care not to sew into the 1/4" seam allowance at the outer edges of the beige diamonds.

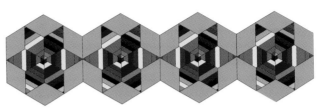

2. Sew a strip panel diamond into each corner between the blocks, sewing from the inner corner to the outside edge.

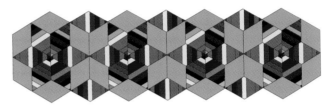

Complete the Table Runner

1. Layer table runner top, batting, and backing.

2. Quilt as desired. A neutral thread was used to stitch a small feather pattern over the entire top.

3. Bind with dark batik binding strips.

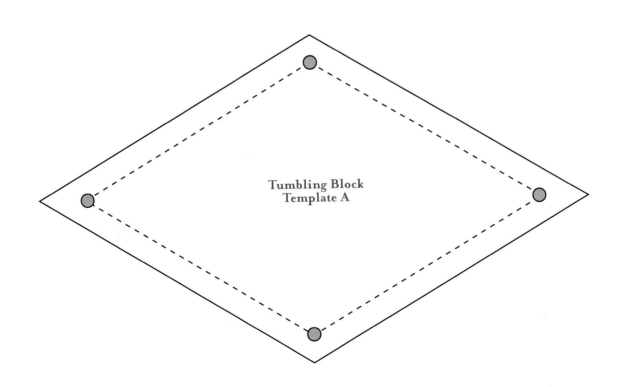

**Tumbling Block
Template A**

Tumbling Block Table Runner

Designed and pieced by Edyta Sitar for Laundry Basket Quilts

Summer Star Quilt

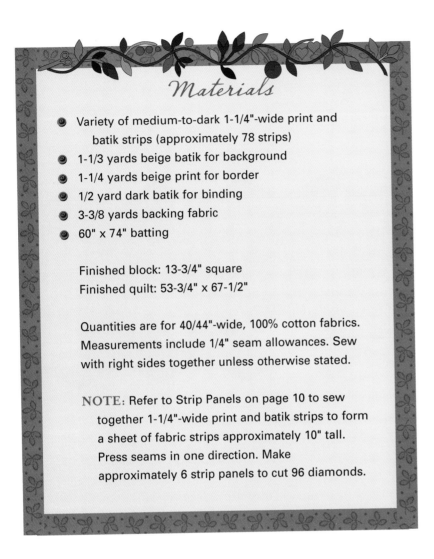

Materials

- Variety of medium-to-dark 1-1/4"-wide print and batik strips (approximately 78 strips)
- 1-1/3 yards beige batik for background
- 1-1/4 yards beige print for border
- 1/2 yard dark batik for binding
- 3-3/8 yards backing fabric
- 60" x 74" batting

Finished block: 13-3/4" square
Finished quilt: 53-3/4" x 67-1/2"

Quantities are for 40/44"-wide, 100% cotton fabrics. Measurements include 1/4" seam allowances. Sew with right sides together unless otherwise stated.

NOTE: Refer to Strip Panels on page 10 to sew together 1-1/4"-wide print and batik strips to form a sheet of fabric strips approximately 10" tall. Press seams in one direction. Make approximately 6 strip panels to cut 96 diamonds.

Cut the Fabrics

From strip panels, cut:

96 diamonds using template A on page 54, positioning the template so the strips run across the width of each diamond as shown

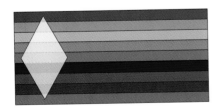

Note: Refer to page 11 to make additional diamonds from the strip panel scraps.

From beige batik, cut:

48 – 4-1/2" squares

12 – 7" squares, cutting each diagonally in an X for a total of 48 triangles

From beige print, cut:

2 – 6-1/2" x 41-3/4" border strips

4 – 6-1/2" x 42" border strips

From dark batik, cut:

6 – 2-1/2" x 42" binding strips

From backing fabric, cut:

2 – 37-1/2" x 60" rectangles

Marking Diamonds

For ease in piecing the Eight-Pointed Star blocks, you may find it helpful to mark the diamonds, squares, and triangles. Use a ruler and pencil to lightly draw a line or dot to indicate the starting and stopping points for the 1/4" set-in seams.

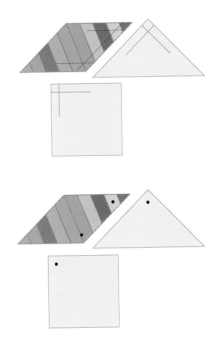

Assemble the Blocks

1. For one Eight-Pointed Star block you will need eight diamonds, four beige batik 4-1/2" squares, and four beige batik triangles.

2. Sew the diamonds together in pairs, stopping at the 1/4" seam allowance mark. Backstitch to secure seam ends. Press all seams in the same direction.

Press

3. Sew together two diamond pairs to make one star half, taking care not to sew into the 1/4" seam allowance. Backstitch to secure seam ends. Trim; press seams in the same direction. Repeat to make a second star half.

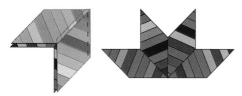

4. Sew the two star halves together. Begin sewing at the center and stop at the marked 1/4" seam allowance, backstitching to secure seam end. Flip the star halves over and complete the seam, sewing again from the center out. Trim and press seams so all are turned in the same direction. Press the seams open to form a tiny pinwheel at the center.

5. Pin a beige batik triangle to one diamond. Sew from the outside edge to the marked inner corner, backstitching to secure at the inner corner. Pin the adjacent diamond to the triangle. Sew from inner corner, backstitching to secure, to the outside edge. Press seams toward the triangle. Repeat to inset the remaining three triangles at the sides of the star.

6. Pin a beige batik 4-1/2" square to one diamond at the corner of the star. Sew from the outside edge to the marked inner corner, backstitching to secure at the

inner corner. Pin the adjacent diamond to the square. Sew from inner corner, backstitching to secure, to the outside edge. Press seams toward the square. Sew beige batik 4-1/2" squares into remaining corners to make an Eight-Pointed Star block.

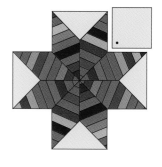

7. Repeat Steps 1-6 to make a total of twelve Eight-Pointed Star blocks.

Make 12

Assemble the Quilt Center

1. Referring to Quilt Center Assembly Diagram, lay out twelve Eight-Pointed Star blocks in four horizontal rows as shown.
2. Sew together blocks in each row. Press seams in one direction, alternating the direction from row to row.
3. Join rows. Press seams in one direction.

Add the Border

1. Referring to Quilt Top Assembly Diagram, sew the 6-1/2" x 41-3/4" border strips to the top and bottom edges of the quilt center. Press seams toward border.
2. Piece the 6-1/2" x 42" border strips to make 2 — 6-1/2" x 67-1/2" side border strips. Sew these to the quilt center. Press seams toward border.

Complete the Quilt

1. Sew together the 37-1/2" x 60" backing rectangles along one long edge, using a 1/2" seam allowance. Press the seam allowance open.
2. Layer quilt top, batting, and pieced backing.
3. Quilt as desired. The entire quilt top was stitched using an all-over large feather pattern.
4. Bind with dark batik binding strips.

Quilt Center Assembly Diagram

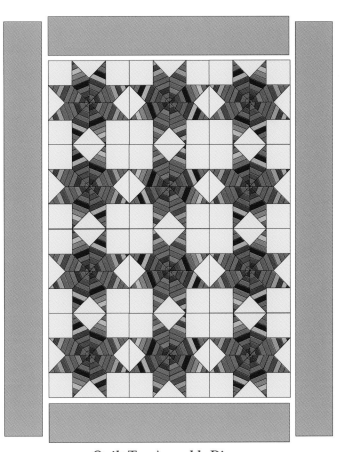

Quilt Top Assembly Diagram

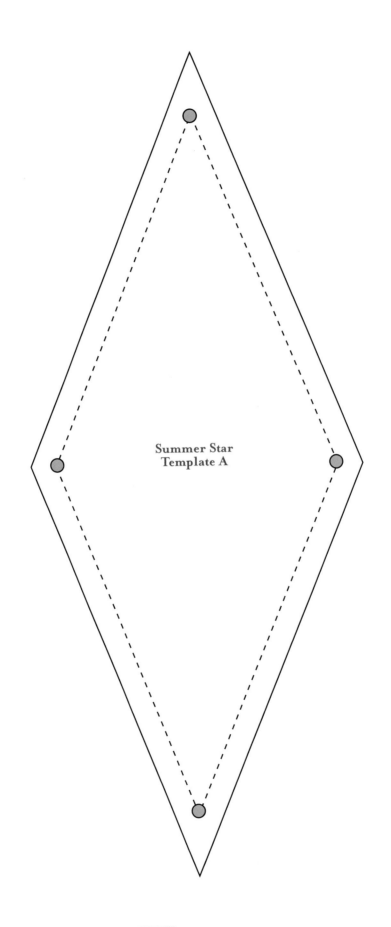

Summer Star
Template A

Summer Star Quilt

Designed and pieced by Edyta Sitar for Laundry Basket Quilts

Sharing Thimbles Quilt

Materials

- Assorted light-to-dark print fabrics to total
  94 – 3-1/2" x 42" fabric strips for trapezoids
- 3/4 yard dark print for binding
- 7-3/8 yards backing fabric
- 110" x 88" batting

Finished quilt: 103-1/2" x 81-1/2"

Quantities are for 40/44"-wide, 100% cotton fabrics.
Measurements include 1/4" seam allowances. Sew
with right sides together unless otherwise stated.

NOTE: For best use of fabric, cut the trapezoid
shapes from 3-1/2"-wide fabric strips; 20
trapezoids can be cut from a 3-1/2" x 42" strip.

Cut the Fabrics

From assorted light-to-dark print strips, cut:

1863 trapezoids using template A on page 58

From dark print, cut:

9 – 2-1/2" x 42" binding strips

From backing, cut:

3 – 37-1/2" x 88" rectangles

Assemble the Quilt Top

1. Referring to the Quilt Center Assembly Diagram, lay out the 1863 trapezoids in horizontal rows with 69 in each of the 27 rows. Take care to position the trapezoids in the direction shown.
2. Sew together the trapezoids in each row; press.
3. Join rows. Press seams in one direction.

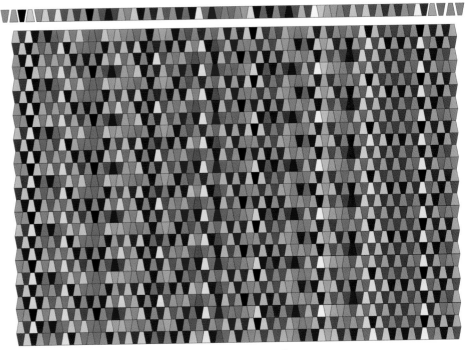

Quilt Center Assembly Diagram

Sharing Thimbles Quilt

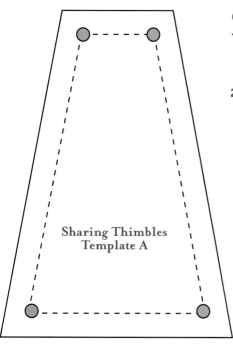

Sharing Thimbles
Template A

Complete the Quilt

1. Trim the left and right edges of the quilt top as shown in the Quilt Top Assembly Diagram.
2. Sew together the 37-1/2" x 88" backing rectangles along the long edges, using a 1/2" seam allowance. Press the seam allowance open.
3. Layer quilt top, batting, and pieced backing.
4. Quilt as desired. The quilt was stitched with neutral thread and a stippling stitch.
5. Bind with dark print binding strips.

Trim   Trim

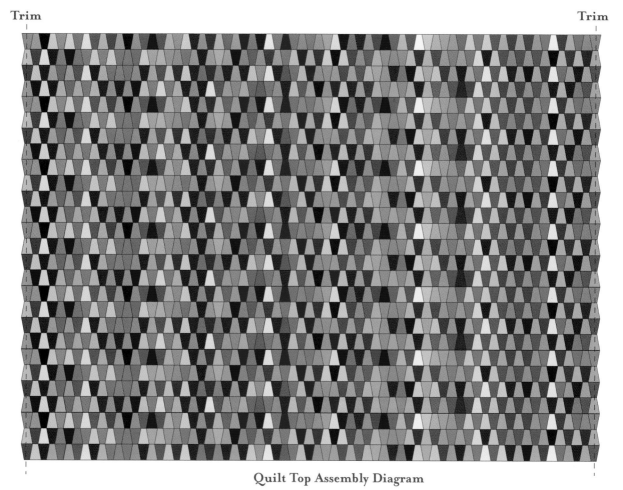

Quilt Top Assembly Diagram

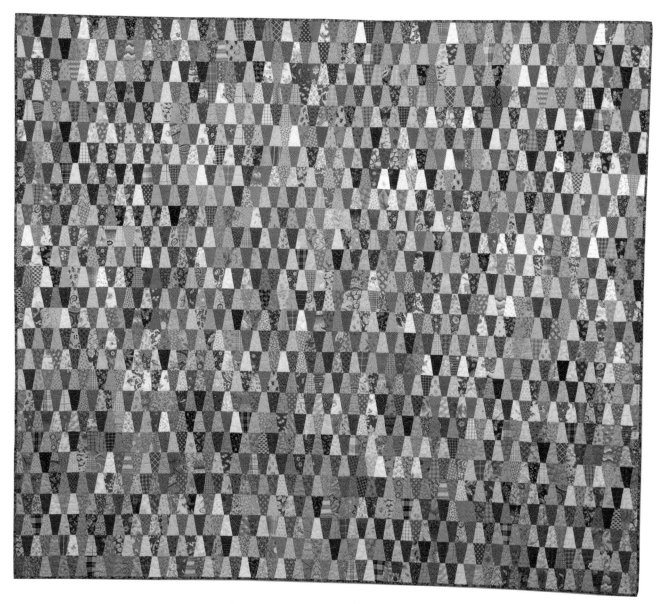

Sharing Thimbles Quilt
Designed and pieced by Edyta Sitar for Laundry Basket Quilts

Spider Star Quilt

Assemble the Quilt Top

1. Referring to the Quilt Top Assembly Diagram, lay out the 152 strip panel triangles and 76 beige print triangles in twelve horizontal rows. Take care to position the strip panel triangles in the direction shown and to align the straight grain of the beige print triangles with the long edges of the rows.

2. Sew the triangles in each row together; press.

3. Join rows. Press seams in one direction.

Cut the Fabrics

From strip panels, cut:

152 triangles using template A on page 62, positioning the template so the strips run across the triangle as shown

From assorted beige prints, cut:

76 triangles using template A on page 62

From medium print, cut:

7 — 2-1/2" x 42" binding strips

From backing, cut:

2 — 28-1/2" x 54" rectangles

Quilt Top Assembly Diagram

Spider Star Quilt

Complete the Quilt

1. Sew together the 28-1/2" x 54" backing rectangles along one long edge, using a 1/2" seam allowance. Press the seam allowance open.

2. Layer quilt top, batting, and pieced backing.

3. Quilt as desired. The quilt was stitched with neutral thread and a stippling stitch.

4. Bind with medium print binding strips.

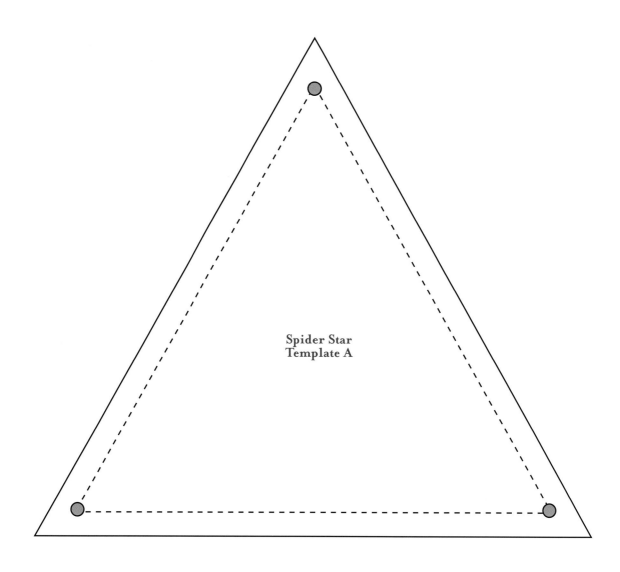

Spider Star Template A

Spider Star Quilt
Designed and pieced by Edyta Sitar for Laundry Basket Quilts

Spool Quilt

Materials

- Variety of medium-to-dark 1"-wide print and batik strips (approximately 40 strips)
- 3-1/4 yards of light batik for block rectangles, blocks, and borders
- 5/8 yard total assorted dark prints and batiks for blocks
- 5/8 yard dark batik for binding
- 3/4 yard total assorted green and blue prints and batiks for leaf appliqués
- 1-1/2 yards total assorted green and brown prints and batiks for vine, bud base, and flower base appliqués
- 1/4 yard total assorted red prints and batiks for flower appliqués
- Assorted pink print scraps for heart appliqués
- Assorted print and batik scraps for berry appliqués
- 3" x 6" rectangle blue batik for scissor appliqué
- 3" x 4" rectangle blue-brown batik for bird appliqué
- 3-7/8 yards backing fabric
- 68" x 77" batting

Finished block: 5" x 6"
Finished quilt: 61-1/2" x 70-1/2"

Quantities are for 40/44"-wide, 100% cotton fabrics. Measurements include 1/4" seam allowances. Sew with right sides together unless otherwise stated.

NOTE: Refer to Strip Panels on page 10 to sew together the medium-to-dark 1-1/2"-wide print and batik strips to form a strip panel approximately 5-1/2" tall. Press seams in one direction. Make approximately 4 strip panels to cut a total of 41—3-1/2" x 4-1/2" rectangles for the thread area of the spools.

Cut the Fabrics

From the strip panels, cut:
41—3-1/2" x 4-1/2" rectangles

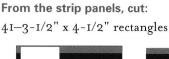

From light batik, cut:
39—5-1/2" x 6-1/2" block rectangles
1—4-1/2" x 6-1/2" block rectangle
1—1-1/2" x 6-1/2" strip
82—1-1/2" x 4-1/2" strips
164—1-1/2" squares
6—8-1/2" x 42" border strips

From assorted dark prints and batiks, cut:
82—1-1/2" x 5-1/2" strips, cutting sets of two matching strips for 40 of the spool blocks and two different strips for the turned block in the bottom right corner

From dark batik, cut:
7—2-1/2" x 42" binding strips

From backing, cut:
2—39" x 68" rectangles

Assemble the Blocks

1. Sew light batik 1-1/2" x 4-1/2" strips to opposite edges of a 3-1/2" x 4-1/2" strip panel rectangle for the thread section. Press seams away from rectangle.

2. Draw a diagonal line across the wrong side of four light batik 1-1/2" squares.

3. Place light batik 1-1/2" squares on the ends of a dark print or batik 1-1/2" x 5-1/2" strip, right sides

64

together, as shown for the top section. Sew on the drawn lines. Trim seams to 1/4" and press seams toward strip. Repeat with the two remaining 1-1/2" squares on a matching dark print or batik 1-1/2" x 5-1/2" strip for the bottom section.

Note: Reserve the trimmed triangles to create the beautiful framed fabric on page 95.

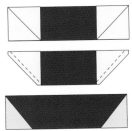

4. Sew the top and bottom sections to the thread section to complete one spool block. Press seams away from thread section.

5. Repeat Steps 1–4 to make a total of 40 spool blocks.

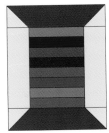

Make 40

6. Make an additional block in the same manner but use two different fabrics for the 1-1/2" x 5-1/2" strips. Add the light batik 1-1/2" x 6-1/2" strip to one edge of this block to complete the turned block for the bottom right corner of the quilt center.

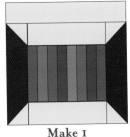

Make 1

Assemble the Quilt Center

1. Referring to Quilt Center Assembly Diagram, lay out 41 spool blocks, 39 light batik 5-1/2" x 6-1/2" block rectangles, and the light batik 4-1/2" x 6-1/2" block rectangle in nine horizontal rows.

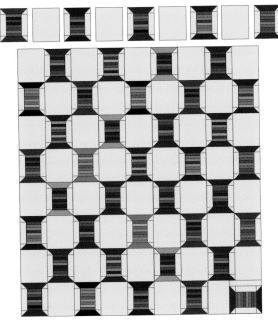

Quilt Center Assembly Diagram

2. Sew together the blocks in each row. Press seams toward block rectangles.

3. Join rows. Press seams in one direction.

Add the Border

1. Piece the 6–8-1/2" x 42" border strips to make the following: 2–8-1/2" x 54-1/2" for sides and 2–8-1/2" x 61-1/2" for top and bottom.

2. Referring to Quilt Top Assembly Diagram, sew side border strips to the quilt center. Press seams toward border. Add the top and bottom border strips to the quilt center. Press seams toward border.

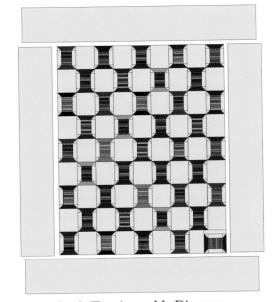

Quilt Top Assembly Diagram

Appliqué the Quilt

Trace the appliqué patterns on pages 68-69. Use the appliqué method of your choice to prepare appliqué pieces.

From green and blue prints and batiks, cut:

42 of pattern A (small leaf)

11 of pattern B (double leaf)

18 of pattern C (large leaf)

20 of pattern C reversed (large leaf)

From green-to-brown prints and batiks, cut:

17 of pattern D (bud base)

6 of pattern E (flower base)

13 of pattern F (vine)

13 of pattern F reversed (vine)

From red prints and batiks, cut:

17 of pattern G (bud)

6 of pattern H (flower)

From pink prints, cut:

8 of pattern I (heart)

From assorted prints and batiks, cut:

7 of pattern J (big berry)

6 each of patterns K and L (medium and small berry)

From blue batik, cut:

1 of pattern M (scissors)

From blue-brown batik, cut:

1 of pattern N (bird)

Position the appliqué pieces on the quilt top, referring to the Appliqué Placement Diagram on page 68 for placement ideas. Arrange the vine pieces on the border, cutting some as needed to curve the vine at the corners of the quilt top and to overlap in the top left corner. Place the remaining appliqué pieces along the vine, cutting lengths from the remaining vine appliqués to create the desired stem length. Appliqué the shapes in place using your favorite method. A narrow buttonhole stitch was used along the edges of each of the appliqué pieces.

Complete the Quilt

1. Sew together the 39" x 68" backing rectangles along one long edge, using a 1/2" seam allowance. Press the seam allowance open.

2. Layer quilt top, batting, and pieced backing.

3. Quilt as desired. Neutral thread was used to stitch closely around the appliqué shapes and each spool. The thread area of each spool is filled with stippling and the background is filled with an allover whimsical design.

4. Bind with dark batik binding strips.

These shapes have been reversed
for fusible appliqué.

Small Leaf (A)
Cut 42

Large Leaf (C)
Cut 18 &
20 reversed

Double Leaf (B)
Cut 11

Bud Base (D)
Cut 17

Flower Base (E)
Cut 6

Bud (G)
Cut 17

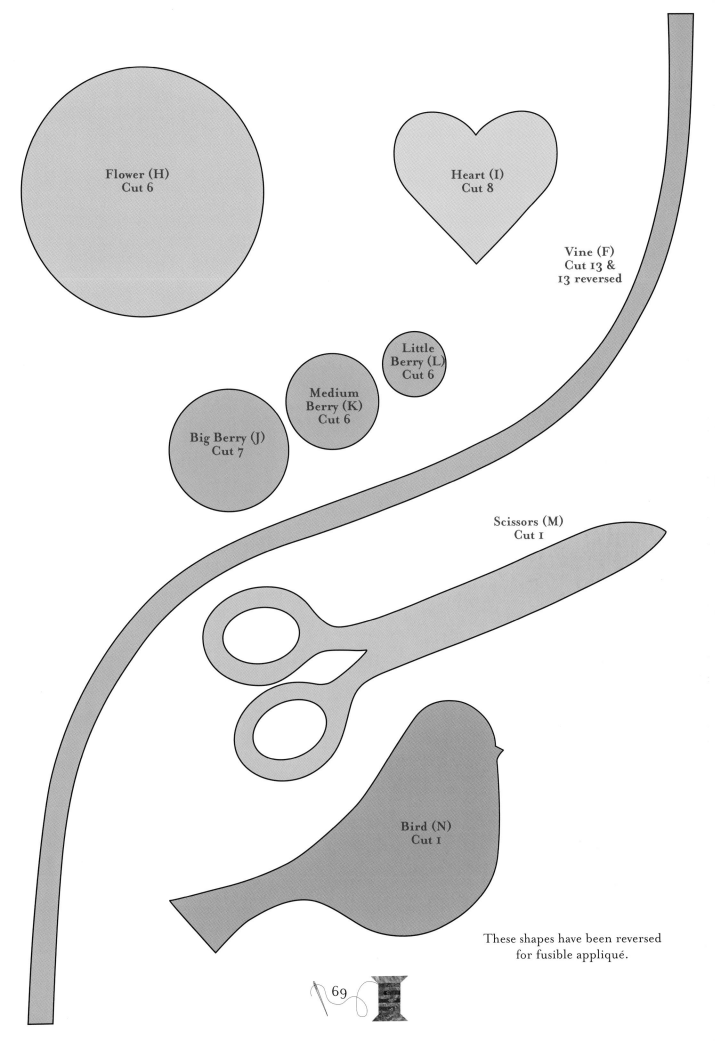

Flower (H)
Cut 6

Heart (I)
Cut 8

Vine (F)
Cut 13 &
13 reversed

Little
Berry (L)
Cut 6

Medium
Berry (K)
Cut 6

Big Berry (J)
Cut 7

Scissors (M)
Cut 1

Bird (N)
Cut 1

These shapes have been reversed
for fusible appliqué.

Spool Quilt

Designed and pieced by Edyta Sitar for Laundry Basket Quilts

Coral Bells Wallhanging

Materials

- Variety of 1"-wide medium-to-dark pink, red, and purple print and batik strips (approximately 24 strips)
- 5/8 yard beige batik for blocks
- 5 or more 9" x 22" pieces (fat eighths) of assorted green prints and batiks for blocks and appliqués
- 1 yard dark red-purple batik for setting triangles, corner triangles, and binding
- 1/2 yard green batik for border
- 42" square backing fabric
- 42" square batting

Finished block: 10" square
Finished wallhanging: 35-1/2" square

Quantities are for 40/44"-wide, 100% cotton fabrics. Measurements include 1/4" seam allowances. Sew with right sides together unless otherwise stated.

NOTE: Refer to Strip Panels on page 10 to sew together the 1"-wide print and batik strips to form a strip panel approximately 6-1/2" tall. Press seams in one direction. Make approximately 2 strip panels to cut 20 diamonds. To create the wallhanging pictured, substitute two diamonds cut from red and purple fabric scraps for two of the strip panel diamonds in the center block.

Cut the Fabrics

From the fabric strip panels, cut:

20 diamonds using template A on page 77, positioning the template so the strips run across the width of each diamond as shown

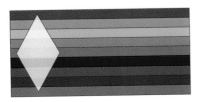

From beige batik, cut:

5 – 5-1/2" squares

12 – triangles using template C on page 77

15 squares using template B on page 77

5 – 2-15/16" squares, cutting each in half diagonally for a total of 10 small triangles

From assorted green prints and batiks, cut:

10 diamonds (five sets of two matching) using template A on page 77; reserve scraps for appliqués

From dark red-purple batik, cut:

1 – 15-3/8" square, cutting it diagonally in an X for a total of 4 setting triangles

2 – 8" squares, cutting each in half diagonally for a total of 4 corner triangles

4 – 2-1/2" x 42" binding strips

From green batik, cut:

4 – 3-1/2" x 40" border strips

Marking Diamonds

For ease in piecing the appliquéd flower blocks, you may find it helpful to mark the diamonds, squares, and triangles. Use a ruler and pencil to lightly draw a line or dot to indicate the starting and stopping points for the 1/4" set-in seams.

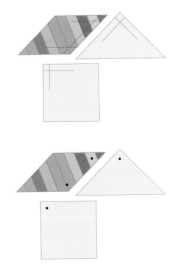

Cut the Appliqués

The instructions that follow are for cutting the appliqués for the 5 appliquéd flower blocks. Trace the appliqué patterns on page 76. Use the appliqué method of your choice to prepare appliqué pieces.

From assorted green print and batik scraps, cut:

5 of pattern A (stem)

5 of pattern B (leaf)

Appliqué and Assemble the Blocks

1. Position matching stem and leaf appliqué pieces on a beige batik 5-1/2" square as shown. The top of the stem will be at a corner of the square so it will be included later in the seams. Appliqué the shapes in place using your favorite method. Repeat to make a total of five appliquéd squares.

2. For each block you will need one appliquéd square, four strip panel diamonds, two matching green diamonds, three beige batik squares cut from template, two beige batik large triangles cut from template, and two beige batik small triangles.

3. Sew the strip panel diamonds together in pairs, stopping at the 1/4" seam allowance mark. Backstitch to secure seam ends. Sew the pairs together in the same manner for the petal half. Trim; press all seams in the same direction.

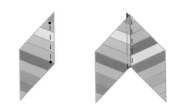

4. Pin a beige batik large triangle to one diamond in a diamond pair. Sew from the outside edge to the marked inner corner, backstitching to secure at the inner corner. Pin the adjacent diamond in the pair to the triangle. Sew from inner corner, backstitching to secure, to the outside edge. Press seams toward the triangle. Repeat to inset a triangle at the second diamond pair.

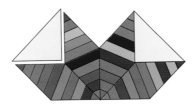

5. Sew the beige batik small triangles to the green diamonds for left and right leaf units as shown. Press seams toward triangles.

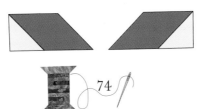

6. Sew the left and right leaf units to the appliquéd square to make the stem half. Press seams in the same direction as the petal half.

7. Sew the petal half and the stem half together. Begin sewing at the center and stop at the marked 1/4" seam allowance, backstitching to secure seam end. Flip the halves over and complete the seam, sewing again from the center out. Trim and press seams so all are turned in the same direction. Press the seams flat and open at the center of the block.

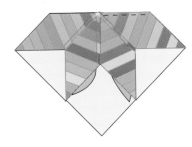

8. Pin a beige batik square to one diamond at the corner between the two petal pairs. Sew from the outside edge to the marked inner corner, backstitching to secure at the inner corner. Pin the adjacent diamond to the square. Sew from the inner corner, backstitching to secure, to the outside edge. Press

seams toward the square. Sew beige batik squares into remaining corners to make an appliquéd flower block.

9. Repeat Steps 2–8 to make a total of five appliquéd flower blocks. There will be two unused large triangles.

Make 5

Assemble the Wallhanging Center

1. Referring to Wallhanging Center Assembly Diagram, lay out five appliquéd flower blocks and four dark red-purple batik setting triangles in diagonal rows.

Wallhanging Center Assembly Diagram

2. Sew together pieces in each row. Press seams in one direction, alternating the direction from row to row.

3. Join rows. Press seams in one direction. Add dark red-purple corner triangles to complete the wallhanging center. Press seams toward corner triangles.

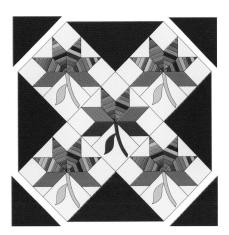

Add the Border

1. Center and sew a green batik 3-1/2" x 40" border strip to one edge of the wallhanging center, beginning and ending the seam

1/4" from the corners of the wallhanging center. Attach a border to each edge of the wallhanging center in the same manner. Press seams toward the border.

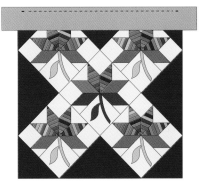

2. Place wallhanging right side up on your ironing board. Working with one corner at a time, extend the border ends out so the vertical strip overlaps the horizontal strip.

3. Lift up the vertical strip and fold it under itself at a 45-degree angle. Check the angle with a ruler and press.

4. With right sides together, fold the wallhanging on the diagonal so the edges of the two border strips line up. Pin and sew along the creased line from the inner point where the previous stitching ends to the outer edge of the border, backstitching to secure. Trim seam to 1/4". Press seam allowance open.

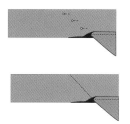

5. Repeat Steps 2-4 for remaining corners.

Complete the Wallhanging

1. Layer wallhanging top, batting, and backing.

2. Quilt as desired. The wallhanging was quilted using neutral thread, stitched closely around the appliqué shapes and in-the-ditch of each diamond. Veins were stitched at the center of the green leaf diamonds and appliquéd leaves and swirls at the center of each flower petal. A feather pattern covers the border, extends over the setting triangles, and onto the corner triangles and outer corners of the blocks. The block background and remaining area of the setting and corner triangles is filled with stippling.

3. Bind with dark red-purple batik binding strips.

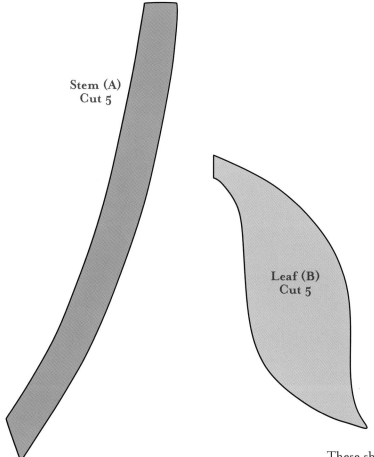

Stem (A)
Cut 5

Leaf (B)
Cut 5

These shapes have been reversed for fusible appliqué.

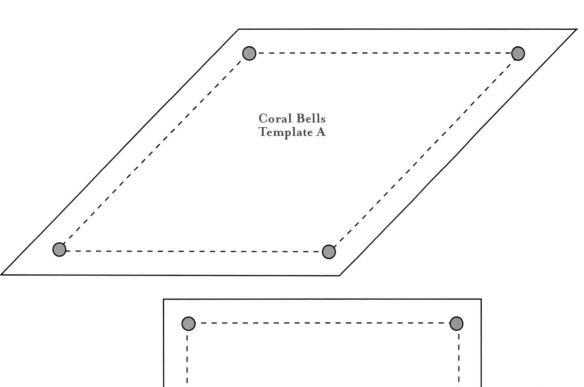

**Coral Bells
Template A**

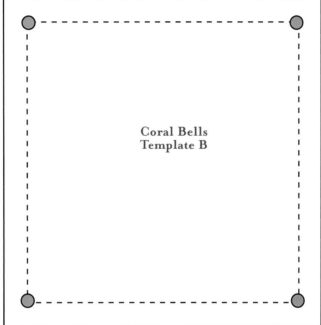

**Coral Bells
Template B**

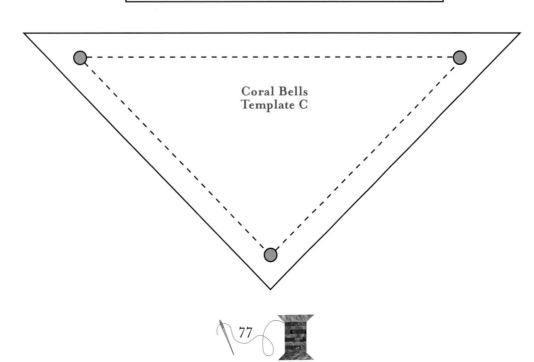

**Coral Bells
Template C**

Coral Bells Wallhanging

Designed and pieced by Edyta Sitar for Laundry Basket Quilts

Coral Bells Quilt

Materials

- Variety of 1"-wide medium-to-dark pink, red, and purple print and batik strips (approximately 72 strips)
- 3-3/4 yards beige batik for blocks, setting squares, and border
- 18 – 9" x 22" pieces (fat eighth) of assorted green prints and batiks for blocks, appliqués, and binding
- 4-3/4 yards backing fabric
- 63" x 83" batting

Finished block: 10" square
Finished quilt: 56-1/2" x 76-1/2"

Quantities are for 40/44"-wide, 100% cotton fabrics. Measurements include 1/4" seam allowances. Sew with right sides together unless otherwise stated.

NOTE: Refer to Strip Panels on page 10 to sew together the 1"-wide print and batik strips to form a strip panel approximately 6-1/2" tall. Press seams in one direction. Make approximately 6 strip panels to cut 72 diamonds. To create the quilt pictured, substitute diamonds cut from red and purple fabric scraps for some of the strip panel diamonds.

Cut the Fabrics

From the strip panels, cut:

72 diamonds using template A on page 84, positioning the template so the strips run across the width of each diamond as shown

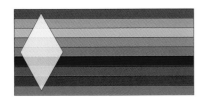

From beige batik, cut:

17 – 10-1/2" setting squares

18 – 5-1/2" squares

36 – triangles using template C on page 84

54 squares using template B on page 84

18 – 2-15/16" squares, cutting each in half diagonally for a total of 36 small triangles

7 – 3-1/2" x 42" border strips

From assorted green prints and batik fat eighths, cut:

2-1/2"-wide strips to total 280" of binding

36 diamonds (18 sets of two matching) using template A on page 84; reserve scraps for appliqués

From backing, cut:

2 – 32" x 83" rectangles

Marking Diamonds

For ease in piecing the appliquéd flower blocks, you may find it helpful to mark the diamonds, squares, and triangles. Use a ruler and pencil to lightly draw a line or dot to indicate the starting and stopping points for the 1/4" set-in seams.

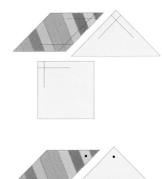

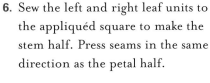

Cut the Appliqués

The instructions that follow are for cutting the appliqués for the 18 appliquéd flower blocks. Trace the appliqué patterns on page 84. Use the appliqué method of your choice to prepare appliqué pieces.

From assorted green print and batik scraps, cut:

18 of pattern A (stem)

18 of pattern B (leaf)

Appliqué and Assemble the Blocks

1. Position matching stem and leaf appliqué pieces on a beige batik 5-1/2" square as shown. The top of the stem will be at a corner of the square so it will be included later in the seams. Appliqué the shapes in place using your favorite method. Repeat to make a total of 18 appliquéd squares.

2. For each block you will need one appliquéd square, four strip panel diamonds, two matching green diamonds, three beige batik squares cut from template, two beige batik large triangles cut from template, and two beige batik small triangles.

3. Sew the strip panel diamonds together in pairs, stopping at the 1/4" seam allowance mark. Backstitch to secure seam ends. Sew the pairs together in the same manner for the petal half. Trim; press all seams in the same direction.

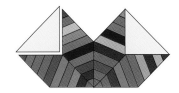

4. Pin a beige batik large triangle to one diamond in a diamond pair. Sew from the outside edge to the marked inner corner, backstitching to secure at the inner corner. Pin the adjacent diamond in the pair to the triangle. Sew from inner corner, backstitching to secure, to the outside edge. Press seams toward the triangle. Repeat to inset a triangle at the second diamond pair.

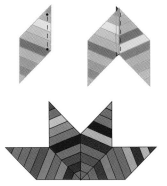

5. Sew the beige batik small triangles to the green diamonds for left and right leaf units as shown. Press seams toward triangles.

6. Sew the left and right leaf units to the appliquéd square to make the stem half. Press seams in the same direction as the petal half.

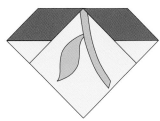

7. Sew the petal half and the stem half together. Begin sewing at the center and stop at the marked 1/4" seam allowance, backstitching to secure seam end. Flip the halves over and complete the seam, sewing again from the center out. Trim and press seams so all are turned in the same direction. Press the seams flat and open at the center of the block.

8. Pin a beige batik square to one diamond at the corner between the two petal pairs. Sew from the outside edge to the marked inner corner, backstitching to secure at the inner corner. Pin the adjacent diamond to the square. Sew from the inner corner, backstitching to secure, to the outside edge. Press seams toward the square. Sew beige batik

squares cut from template into remaining corners to make an appliquéd flower block.

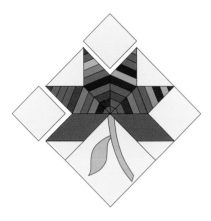

9. Repeat Steps 2–8 to make a total of 18 appliquéd flower blocks.

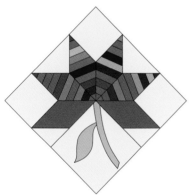

Make 18

Assemble the Quilt Center

1. Referring to Quilt Center Assembly Diagram, lay out 18 appliquéd flower blocks and 17 beige batik 10-3/4" setting squares in seven horizontal rows as shown.
2. Sew together pieces in each row. Press seams toward the setting squares.
3. Join rows. Press seams in one direction.

Quilt Center Assembly Diagram

Add the Border

1. Piece the 3-1/2" x 42" border strips to make the following:
   2 — 3-1/2" x 50-1/2" for top and bottom and
   2 — 3-1/2" x 76-1/2" for sides.

2. Referring to Quilt Top Assembly Diagram, sew top and bottom border strips to the quilt center. Press seams toward border. Add the side border strips to the quilt center. Press seams toward border.

Quilt Top Assembly Diagram

Complete the Quilt

1. Sew together the 32" x 83" backing rectangles along one long edge, using a 1/2" seam allowance. Press the seam allowance open.
2. Layer quilt top, batting, and pieced backing.
3. Quilt as desired. Neutral thread was used to stitch closely around the appliqué shapes and in-the-ditch of each diamond. Veins were stitched at the center of the green leaf diamonds and swirls at the center of each flower petal. A feather pattern covers the border and extends onto the blocks. There is an XXX motif in the block squares and the background of the appliquéd flower blocks is filled with stippling.
4. Bind with green print and batik binding strips.

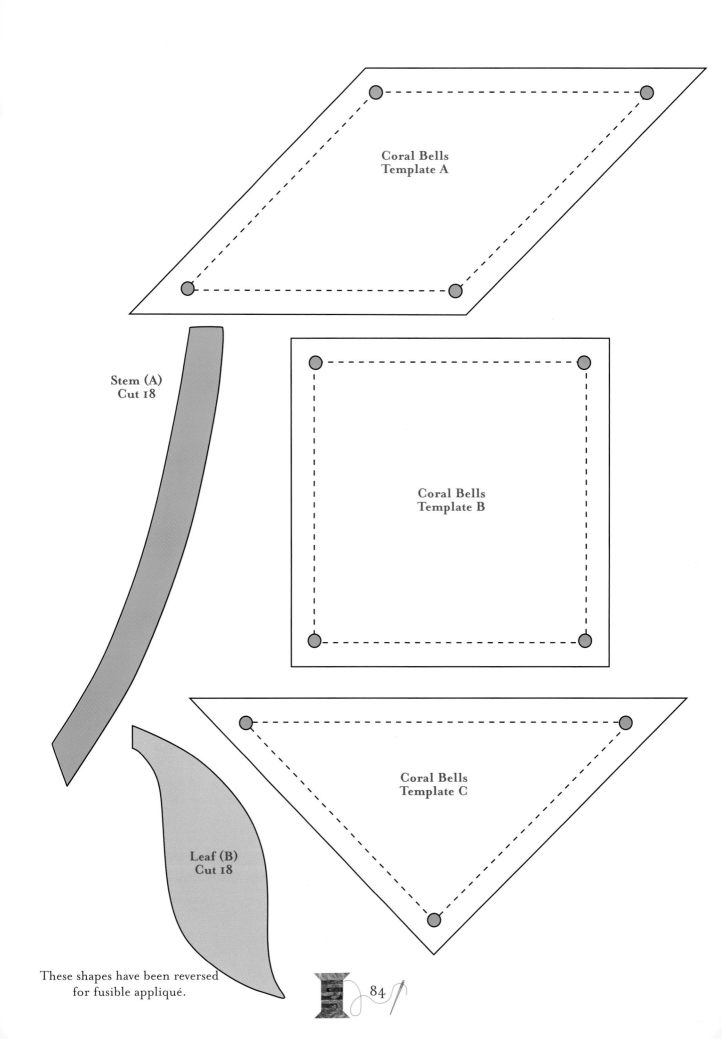

Coral Bells
Template A

Stem (A)
Cut 18

Coral Bells
Template B

Coral Bells
Template C

Leaf (B)
Cut 18

These shapes have been reversed
for fusible appliqué.

Coral Bells Quilt

Designed and pieced by Edyta Sitar for Laundry Basket Quilts

Wishing Well Quilt

Materials

- Variety of 1-1/4" and 1-1/2"-wide medium-to-dark print and batik strips (approximately 72 strips)
- 1-2/3 yards variety of light prints and batiks for block centers
- 1/3 yard beige print for border
- 1/2 yard dark print for binding
- Quarter-square triangle ruler or 8" or larger square ruler
- 3 yards backing fabric
- 51" square batting

Finished block: 10" square
Finished quilt: 44-1/2" square

Quantities are for 40/44"-wide, 100% cotton fabrics. Measurements include 1/4" seam allowances. Sew with right sides together unless otherwise stated.

NOTE: Refer to Strip Panels on page 10 to sew together the 1-1/4" and 1-1/2"-wide print and batik strips to form a strip panel approximately 12" tall. Press seams in one direction. Make approximately 6 strip panels to cut a total of 64 – 3-3/4" x 12" segments.

Cut the Fabrics

From strip panels, cut:
64 – 3-3/4" x 12" segments with the strips running across the rectangles as shown

3-3/4"

From light prints and batiks, cut:
64 – 3" x 12" strips
From beige print, cut:
4 – 2-1/2" x 42-1/2" border strips
From dark print, cut
5 – 2-1/2" x 42" binding strips
From backing, cut:
2 – 26" x 51" rectangles

Assemble the Blocks

1. Sew a light print or batik 3" x 12" strip to one long edge of each 3-3/4" x 12" strip panel rectangle as shown. Press seams toward the light print or batik strip.

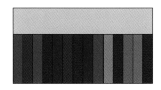

2. Position the ruler on the pieced fabric from Step 1, aligning the 8s on the ruler with the remaining long edge of the fabric strip rectangle. Cut along the edges of the ruler for one triangle. Repeat to cut 64 triangles.

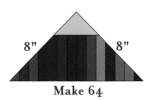

8"   8"

Make 64

3. Lay out four triangles as shown. Sew together the triangles in pairs. Press seams in opposite directions. Join the pairs to make a block. Press seams in one direction. Repeat to make a total of 16 blocks.

Make 16

Wishing Well Quilt

Assemble the Quilt Center

1. Referring to Quilt Center Assembly Diagram, lay out 16 blocks in four horizontal rows.

2. Sew together the blocks in each row. Press seams in one direction, alternating the direction from row to row.

3. Join rows. Press seams in one direction.

Add the Border

1. Use a partial seam to sew one light print 2-1/2" x 42-1/2" border strip to the top of the quilt center, stopping several inches from the right edge of the quilt center as shown. Press seams toward border.

2. Add the next two border strips to the quilt center in a counter-clockwise direction as shown, pressing seams toward the border.

3. Sew the final border strip to the quilt center and press. Complete the partial seam at the top of the quilt center, connecting the top and right border strips.

Complete the Quilt

1. Sew together the 26" x 51" backing rectangles along one long edge, using a 1/2" seam allowance. Press the seam allowance open.

2. Layer quilt top, batting, and pieced backing.

3. Quilt as desired. The quilt was stitched using neutral thread for an allover swirl pattern.

4. Bind with dark print binding strips.

Quilt Center Assembly Diagram

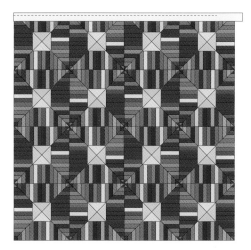

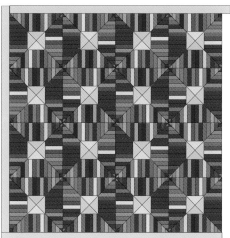

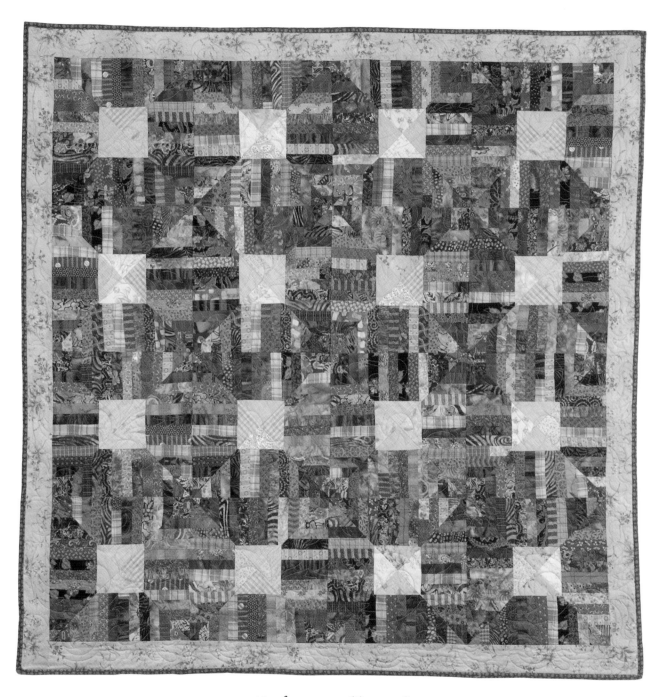

Wishing Well Quilt

Designed and pieced by Edyta Sitar for Laundry Basket Quilts

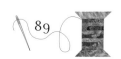

Treasure Box Table Topper

Materials

- Variety of light-to-dark 1"-1-1/2"-wide print and batik strips (approximately 96 strips)
- 3/8 yard blue batik for binding
- 1-1/8 yards backing fabric
- 42" x 38" batting

Finished block: 5" hexagon
Finished table topper: 35-1/2" x 32"

Quantities are for 40/44"-wide, 100% cotton fabrics. Measurements include 1/4" seam allowances. Sew with right sides together unless otherwise stated.

NOTE: Refer to Strip Panels on page 10 to sew together the 1"-1-1/2"-wide print and batik strips to form a strip panel approximately 7" tall. Press seams in one direction. Make approximaately 12 strip panels to cut 144 diamonds and 6 triangles.

Cut the Fabrics

From the strip panels, cut:

144 diamonds using template A on page 93, positioning the template so the strips run across the width of each diamond as shown

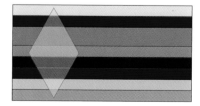

6 triangles using template B on page 93

From blue batik, cut:

5 — 2-1/2" x 42" binding strips

From backing, cut:

1 — 42" x 38" rectangle

Marking Diamonds

For ease in piecing the blocks, you may find it helpful to mark all the diamonds and triangles. Use a ruler and pencil to lightly draw a line or dot to indicate the starting and stopping points for the 1/4" set-in seams.

Assemble the Blocks

1. Lay out three strip panel diamonds as shown.

2. Sew the two lower diamonds together in a pair. Start and stop sewing at the 1/4" seam allowance marks and backstitch to secure seam ends. Press seams to the left.

3. Pin the third diamond to one of the diamonds in the pair. Sew between the marks and backstitch to secure at each end. Pin the adjacent diamond in the pair to the third diamond. Sew from the inner corner to the outside mark, backstitching to secure at each end to make one block. Press seams toward the third diamond.

4. Repeat Steps 1-3 to make a total of 46 blocks.

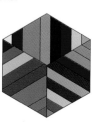

Make 46

5. Sew the strip panel triangles to the remaining strip panel diamonds to make three left partial blocks and three right partial blocks as shown. Press seams toward the diamonds.

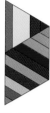

Make 3   Make 3

Assemble the Table Topper

1. Referring to the Table Topper Assembly Diagram, lay out the 46 blocks, three left partial blocks, and three right partial blocks in seven horizontal rows.
2. Sew together the blocks and partial blocks in each row, starting and stopping stitching at the 1/4" marks and backstitching to secure

the thread ends. Press seams to the right.

3. Join the rows in the same manner.

Complete the Table Topper

1. Layer table topper top, batting, and backing.
2. Quilt as desired. The table topper was stitched using neutral thread for an allover swirl pattern.
3. Bind with blue batik binding strips.

Table Topper Assembly Diagram

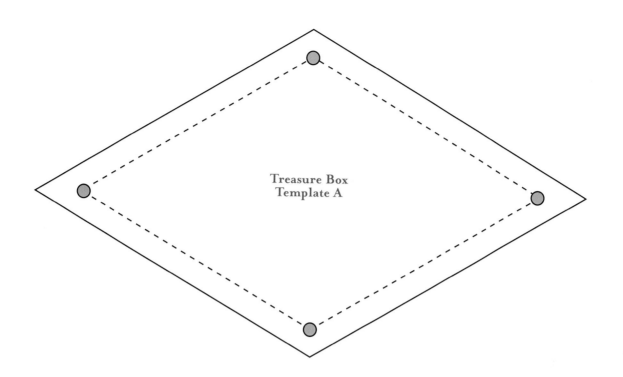

Treasure Box
Template A

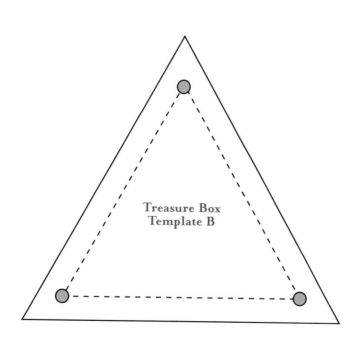

Treasure Box
Template B

Treasure Box Table Topper
Designed and pieced by Edyta Sitar for Laundry Basket Quilts

Close to My Heart By Laundry Basket Quilts for *moda* © modafabrics.com 100%

Here's a Tip

Use the leftover half-square triangles from the Spools Quilt on page 64 to create a
beautiful framed fabric piece.

Family Estate Wallhanging

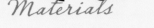

Materials

- Variety of medium-to-dark 1"-wide print and batik strips (approximately 7 strips)
- 1/2 yard beige batik for block and inner border
- 10-1/2" x 3-1/2" rectangle of dark print for roof
- 14 assorted dark print and batik scraps for inner border
- 1/8 yard dark red batik for middle border
- 1/3 yard dark print for outer border
- 1/4 yard red batik for binding
- 3" x 6" rectangle of dark print for door appliqué
- 5" square of light print for window appliqués
- 2–5" x 12" rectangles of assorted brown prints and batiks for branch appliqués
- 8–2" x 4" rectangles of assorted green/brown prints and batiks for leaf and wing appliqués
- 3" x 6" rectangle blue batik for bird body appliqué
- 2-1/2" square of red batik for heart appliqué
- 2" square of rust print for berry
- Black embroidery floss
- Embroidery needle
- Black fabric marker
- 32" square backing fabric
- 32" square batting

Finished block: 10" square
Finished wallhanging: 25-1/2" square

Quantities are for 40/44"-wide, 100% cotton fabrics. Measurements include 1/4" seam allowances. Sew with right sides together unless otherwise stated.

NOTE: Refer to Strip Panels on page 10 to sew together the medium-to-dark 1"-wide print and batik strips to form a strip panel approximately 8-1/2" tall. Make the panel large enough to cut a 10-1/2" x 7-1/2" rectangle for the house front. Press seams in one direction.

Cut the Fabrics

From strip panel, cut:

1 – 10-1/2" x 7-1/2" rectangle with the strips running lengthwise

From beige batik, cut:

2 – 3-1/2" squares

14 – 3-1/4" squares, cutting each diagonally in an X for a total of 56 inner border triangles

2 – 2-1/2" x 10-1/2" strips

2 – 2-1/2" x 14-1/2" strips

4 – 2-1/2" squares

From assorted dark print and batik scraps, cut:

14 – 3-1/4" squares, cutting each diagonally in an X for a total of 56 inner border triangles

Note: If you made the Farmhouse Quilt on page 16, use the reserved roof section triangles for the inner border of the Family Estate Wallhanging.

From dark red batik, cut:

2 – 1" x 18-1/2" middle border strips

2 – 1" x 19-1/2" middle border strips

From dark print, cut:

2 – 3-1/2" x 19-1/2" outer border strips

2 – 3-1/2" x 25-1/2" outer border strips

From red batik, cut:

3 – 2-1/2" x 42" binding strips

Cut the Appliqués

Trace the appliqué patterns on page 100. Use the appliqué method of your choice to prepare appliqué pieces.

From medium-to-dark print, cut:

1 – 2" x 5-1/2" door appliqué

From light print, cut:

2 – 2" square window appliqués

From brown print and batik, cut:

1 of pattern D (branch)

1 of pattern D reversed (branch)

From assorted green/brown prints and batiks, cut:

3 of pattern C (leaf)

3 of pattern C reversed (leaf)

1 of pattern E (bird wing)

2 of pattern A (small leaf)

From blue batik, cut:

1 of pattern F (bird)

From red batik, cut:

1 of pattern B (heart)

From rust print, cut:

1 of pattern G (flower)

Assemble the Farmhouse Block

1. Draw a diagonal line across the wrong side of two beige batik 3-1/2" squares.

2. Place light batik 3-1/2" squares right sides together on the top corners of the dark print 10-1/2" x 3-1/2" rectangle as shown for the roof section. Sew on the drawn lines. Trim seams to 1/4" and press seams toward the triangles.

3. Sew the roof section to the 10-1/2" x 7-1/2" strip panel rectangle. Press seams toward roof section.

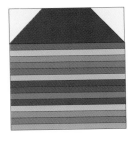

4. Position the door and window appliqué pieces on the house front, aligning the bottom edges of the door and the fabric strip rectangle. Appliqué in place using your favorite method.

5. Sew the beige batik 2-1/2" x 10-1/2" strips to the left and right edges of the farmhouse block. Press seams toward beige batik strips. Sew the beige batik 2-1/2" x 14-1/2" strips to the top and bottom edges of the block. Press seams toward beige batik strips.

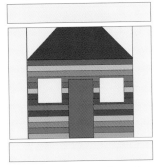

Assemble the Inner Border

1. Referring to the diagram, lay out two beige batik and two matching dark print or batik inner border triangles. Sew the triangles together in pairs. Press the seams toward the dark triangles. Join the pairs together to make one hourglass unit. Press the seams in one direction. Each pieced hourglass unit should measure 2-1/2" square. Repeat to make a total of 28 hourglass units.

Make 28

2. Sew seven hourglass units together in a row to make an inner border unit. Press the seam allowances open. The pieced inner border unit should

measure 2-1/2" x 14-1/2". Repeat to make a total of four inner border units.

Make 4

Add the Borders

1. Sew pieced inner border units to opposite edges of the block. Press seams toward the block.

2. Add beige batik 2-1/2" squares to ends of each remaining inner border unit. Press seams toward beige batik squares. Sew pieced inner borders to remaining edges of the block. Press seams toward the block.

3. Sew dark red batik 1" x 18-1/2" middle border strips to the left and right edges of the wallhanging center. Press seams toward middle border. Sew dark red batik

1" x 19-1/2" middle border strips to the top and bottom edges of the wallhanging center. Press seams toward middle border.

4. Sew dark print 3-1/2" x 19-1/2" outer border strips to the top and bottom edges of the wallhanging center. Press seams toward outer border. Sew dark print 3-1/2" x 25-1/2" outer border strips to the left and right edges of the wallhanging center. Press seams toward outer border.

Appliqué and Embroider the Wallhanging

1. Referring to the Wallhanging Top Diagram as a guide, position the remaining appliqué pieces on the wallhanging top and appliqué the shapes in place using your favorite method.

2. Referring to page 100, use black floss to embroider "Est." and the desired year on the beige batik strip below the house. Backstitch the letters and numbers and make a French knot for the period.

3. Use black floss to make a French knot for the bird's eye. Draw the beak with a black fabric marker.

Complete the Wallhanging

1. Layer wallhanging top, batting, and backing.

2. Quilt as desired. Neutral thread was used to stitch closely around each appliqué shape and along the edges of the farmhouse roof and front. Horizontal lines are stitched in-the-ditch of every other strip of the farmhouse front. The inner border was stitched in-the-ditch along the edges of the beige batik triangles and then echo-quilted 3/8" outside the dark print triangles to create a line of zigzag stitching toward the house. The middle border was stitched in-the-ditch along both edges. The outer border is filled with a swirl pattern.

3. Bind with red batik binding strips.

Wallhanging Top Diagram

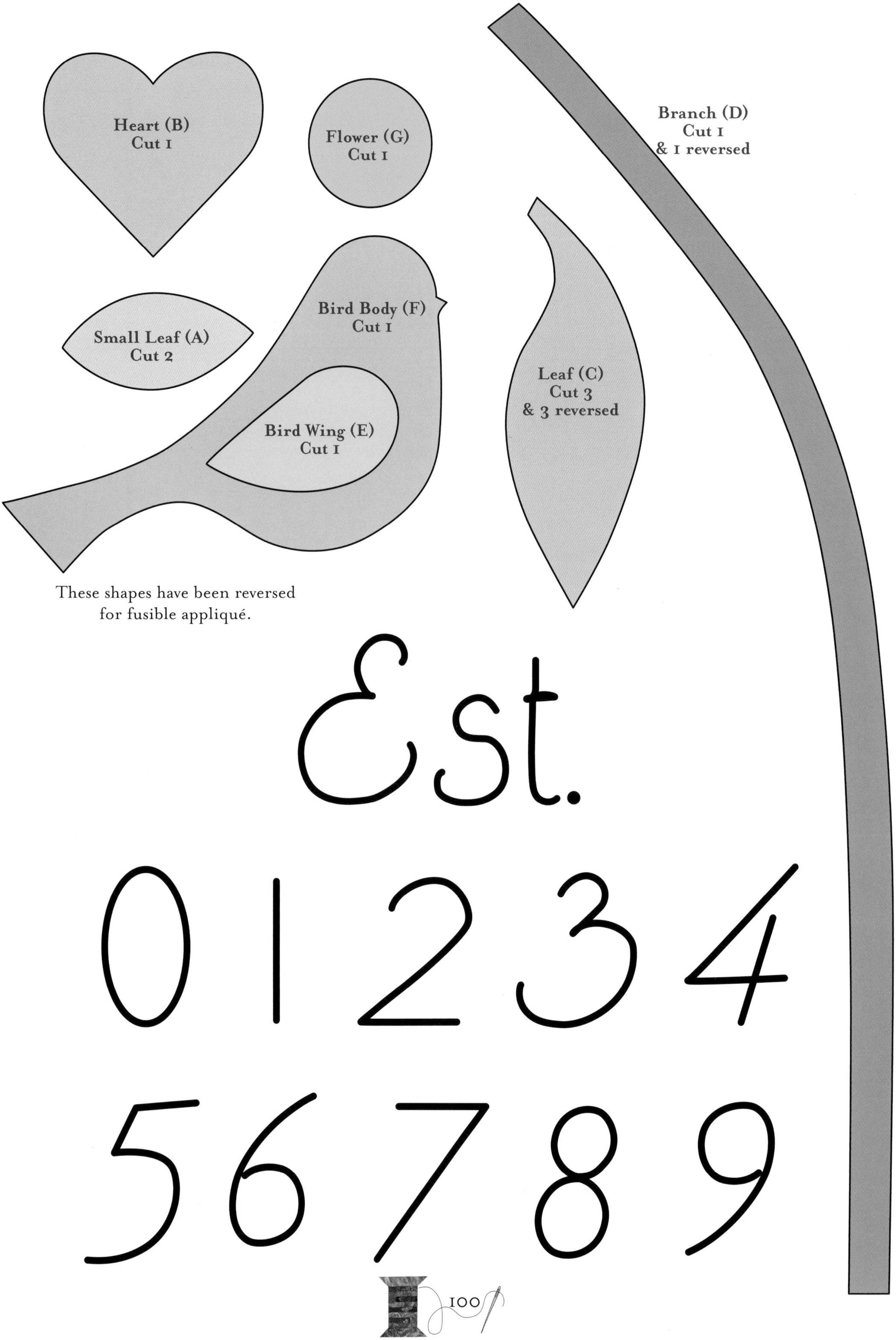

Heart (B)
Cut 1

Flower (G)
Cut 1

Branch (D)
Cut 1
& 1 reversed

Small Leaf (A)
Cut 2

Bird Body (F)
Cut 1

Bird Wing (E)
Cut 1

Leaf (C)
Cut 3
& 3 reversed

These shapes have been reversed
for fusible appliqué.

Est.

0 1 2 3 4

5 6 7 8 9

Est. 1993

Family Estate Wallhanging

Designed and pieced by Edyta Sitar for Laundry Basket Quilts

Blooming Baskets Quilt

Materials

- Variety of 1"-1-1/4"-wide print and batik strips (approximately 28 strips)
- 3 yards beige batik for blocks, setting squares, setting triangles, and corner triangles
- Assorted brown print and batik scraps for blocks
- 1/2 yard total assorted green prints and batiks for leaf appliqués
- 25 – 3" x 6" rectangles of assorted brown prints and batiks for stem appliqués
- 3 – 5" x 12" rectangles of assorted dark brown prints and batiks for branch appliqués
- Assorted pink print scraps for bud appliqués
- Assorted red prints and batik scraps for berry appliqués
- 3 – 3" x 5" rectangles of assorted blue prints and batiks for bird body appliqués
- 3" x 6" rectangle of light brown batik for bird chest appliqués
- Black fabric marker
- 3/8 yard dark print for binding
- 2-5/8 yards backing fabric
- 46" x 65" batting

Finished block: 7" square
Finished quilt: 40" x 59"

Quantities are for 40/44"-wide, 100% cotton fabrics. Measurements include 1/4" seam allowances. Sew with right sides together unless otherwise stated.

NOTE: Refer to Strip Panels on page 10 to sew together the 1"-1-1/4"-wide print and batik strips to form a strip panel approximately 8-1/2" tall. Press seams in one direction. Make approximately 2 strip panels to cut five 7-1/4" squares.

Cut the Fabrics

From the strip panels, cut:

5 – 7-1/4" squares, cutting each diagonally in an X for a total of 20 triangles

From beige batik, cut:

1 – 40" x 9-1/2" rectangle

12 – 7-1/2" setting squares

4 – 11-1/8" squares, cutting each diagonally in an X for a total of 16 setting triangles

10 – 7-7/8" squares, cutting each in half diagonally for a total of 20 large triangles

2 – 5-7/8" squares, cutting each in half diagonally for a total of 4 corner squares

40 – 1-7/8" x 5" rectangles, trim 20 with template A on page 105, then trim remaining 20 with template A reversed

10 – 3-5/8" squares, cutting each in half diagonally for a total of 20 small triangles

From assorted brown print and batik scraps, cut:

20 – 2-1/4" squares, cutting each in half diagonally for a total of 40 triangles

From dark print, cut:

5 – 2-1/2" x 42" binding strips

From backing, cut:

2 – 33" x 46" rectangles

Cut the Appliqués

The instructions that follow are for cutting the appliqués for 19 basket blocks and the top border. Trace the appliqué patterns on page 106. Use the appliqué method of your choice to prepare appliqué pieces.

From assorted green prints and batiks, cut:

22 of pattern B (double leaf)

3 of pattern B reversed (double leaf)

10 of pattern C (small leaf)

2 of pattern D (large leaf)

1 of pattern D reversed (large leaf)

From assorted brown prints and batiks, cut:

3 of pattern E (stem)

3 of pattern E reversed (stem)

19 of pattern L (basket handle)

From dark brown prints and batiks, cut:

1 of pattern F (lower branch)

1 of pattern F reversed (lower branch)

1 of pattern G (upper branch)

Blooming Baskets Quilt

From assorted pink print scraps, cut:

22 of pattern H (bud)

3 of pattern H reversed (bud)

From assorted red prints and batik scraps, cut:

10 of pattern I (berry)

From blue print and batik scraps, cut:

2 of pattern J (bird body)

1 of pattern J reversed (bird body)

From light brown batik, cut:

2 of pattern K (bird chest)

1 of pattern K reversed (bird chest)

Appliqué and Assemble the Basket Blocks

1. Position basket handle, leaf, and bud appliqué pieces on a beige batik large triangle as shown. Align the bottom edges of the basket handle and the triangle so the stem end will be included later in the seam. Appliqué the shapes in place using your favorite method. Repeat to make a total of 19 appliquéd triangles.

2. Lay out one appliquéd triangle, one fabric strip triangle, two beige batik A pieces, two matching brown print or batik triangles, and one beige batik small triangle as shown.

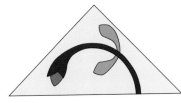

3. Sew brown print or batik triangles to the beige batik A pieces for left and right side sections. Press seams toward A. Sew these to the fabric strip triangle; press seams toward side sections.

4. Add the beige batik small triangle to the bottom of the basket to complete the basket section. Press seam toward beige batik triangle. Join the basket section and appliquéd triangle to complete one block.

5. Repeat Steps 2-4 to make a total of 19 appliquéd basket blocks.

Make 19

6. Substitute the remaining beige batik large triangle for the appliquéd triangle to make the 20th block.

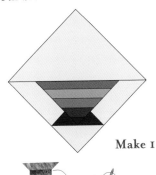

Make 1

Assemble the Quilt Top

1. Referring to Quilt Top Assembly Diagram, lay out 19 appliquéd basket blocks, one basket block, 12 beige batik 7-1/2" setting squares, and 14 beige batik setting triangles in diagonal rows as shown. There will be two unused setting triangles.

2. Sew together pieces in each row. Press seams toward the setting pieces.

3. Join rows. Press seams in one direction. Add beige batik corner triangles; press seams toward the corner triangles. Add the beige batik 40" x 9-1/2" top border rectangle to complete the quilt top. Press seams toward top border.

4. Referring to diagram on page 105 as a guide, position the remaining appliqué pieces on the quilt top and appliqué the shapes in place using your favorite method.

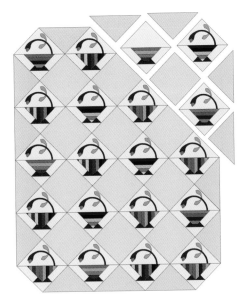

Quilt Top Assembly Diagram

Complete the Quilt

1. Sew together the 33" x 46" backing rectangles along one long edge, using a 1/2" seam allowance. Press the seam allowance open.

2. Layer quilt top, batting, and pieced backing.

3. Quilt as desired. Neutral thread was used to stitch closely around each appliqué shape and along the edges of the basket pieces. Additionally, every other fabric strip of the basket was stitched in-the-ditch. There is a whimsical design in the block squares and the background of the appliquéd basket blocks, the setting triangles, the corner squares, and the top border is filled with stippling.

4. Use a black fabric marker to draw a beak and eye for each bird.

5. Bind with dark print binding strips.

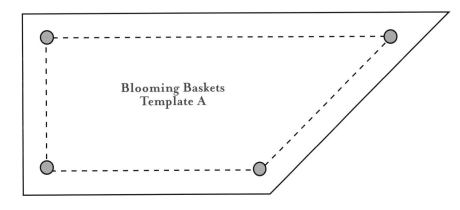

**Blooming Baskets
Template A**

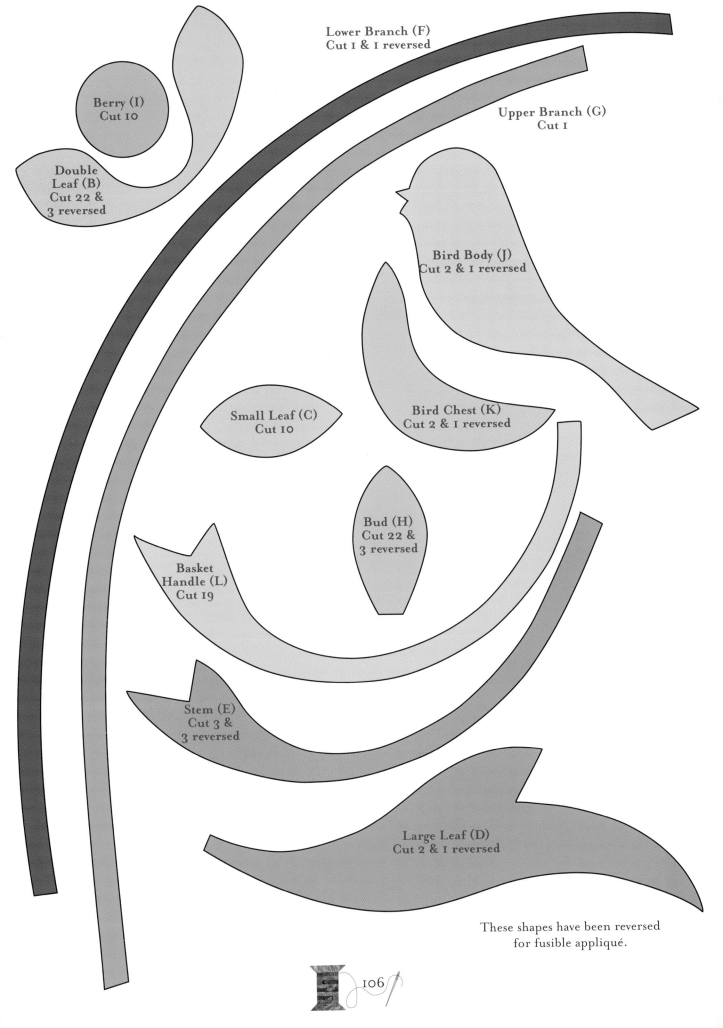

Berry (I)
Cut 10

Double
Leaf (B)
Cut 22 &
3 reversed

Lower Branch (F)
Cut 1 & 1 reversed

Upper Branch (G)
Cut 1

Bird Body (J)
Cut 2 & 1 reversed

Small Leaf (C)
Cut 10

Bird Chest (K)
Cut 2 & 1 reversed

Bud (H)
Cut 22 &
3 reversed

Basket
Handle (L)
Cut 19

Stem (E)
Cut 3 &
3 reversed

Large Leaf (D)
Cut 2 & 1 reversed

These shapes have been reversed
for fusible appliqué.

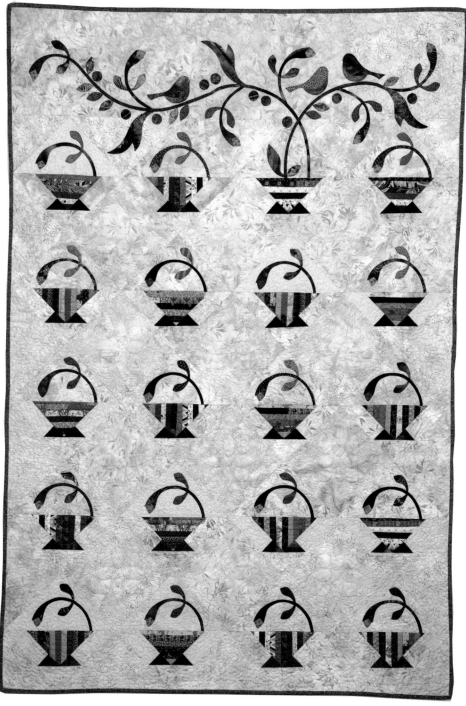

Blooming Baskets Quilt
Designed and pieced by Edyta Sitar for Laundry Basket Quilts

Little Bits Quilt

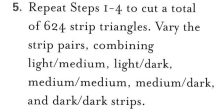

Materials

- Assorted 1-5/8"-wide light-to-dark print strips (approximately 90 strips)
- 4 yards assorted light-to-dark print fabrics
- Quarter-square triangle ruler or 6" or larger square ruler
- 5/8 yard green print for binding
- 4-3/8 yards backing fabric
- 78" x 84" batting

Finished block: 6" square
Finished quilt: 72" x 78"

Quantities are for 40/44"-wide, 100% cotton fabrics. Measurements include 1/4" seam allowances. Sew with right sides together unless otherwise stated.

Cut the Fabrics

From assorted light-to-dark prints, cut:

312 – 4-1/4" squares, cutting each diagonally in an X for a total of 1248 quarter-triangles

From green print, cut:

8 – 2-1/2" x 42" binding strips

From backing, cut:

2 – 42-1/2" x 78" rectangles

Make the Strip Triangles

1. Sew two 1-5/8"-wide strips together in a pair as shown.

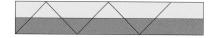

2. Position the ruler on the strip pair, aligning the 3-7/8" marks on the ruler with one long edge of the pair. Cut along the diagonal edges of the ruler for one strip triangle.

3. Turn the ruler to align the 3-7/8" marks with the opposite edge of the strip pair. Cut along one diagonal edge of the ruler for the second strip triangle.

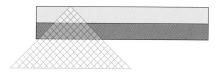

4. Continue in this manner, cutting as many strip triangles as possible from the strip pair.

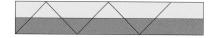

5. Repeat Steps 1-4 to cut a total of 624 strip triangles. Vary the strip pairs, combining light/medium, light/dark, medium/medium, medium/dark, and dark/dark strips.

Assemble the Blocks

1. For one block you will need four strip triangles and eight quarter-triangles. Vary the quarter-triangles to combine light/medium, light/dark, and medium/dark quarter-triangles as desired.

2. Sew the quarter-triangles together in pairs as shown to make 4 pairs. Press seams in one direction.

3. Sew together a strip triangle and a quarter-triangle pair from Step 2 as shown to make a pieced triangle-square. Press the seams toward the strip triangle. Repeat to make a total of four pieced triangle-squares.

4. Lay out the four pieced triangle-squares as shown. Sew the pieced triangle-squares together in rows. Press the seams in opposite directions. Sew the rows together to complete one block; press.

Little Bits Quilt

5. Repeat Steps 1-4 to make a total of 156 blocks.

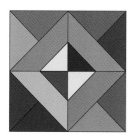

Make 156

Assemble the Quilt Top

1. Referring to Quilt Top Assembly Diagram, lay out 156 blocks in 13 horizontal rows of 12 blocks.
2. Sew the blocks in each row together. Press seams in one direction, alternating the direction from row to row.
3. Join rows. Press seams in one direction.

Complete the Quilt

1. Sew together the 42-1/2" x 78" backing rectangles along one long edge, using a 1/2" seam allowance. Press the seam allowance open.
2. Layer quilt top, batting, and pieced backing.
3. Quilt as desired. The quilt was stitched with neutral thread and a stippling stitch.
4. Bind with green print binding strips.

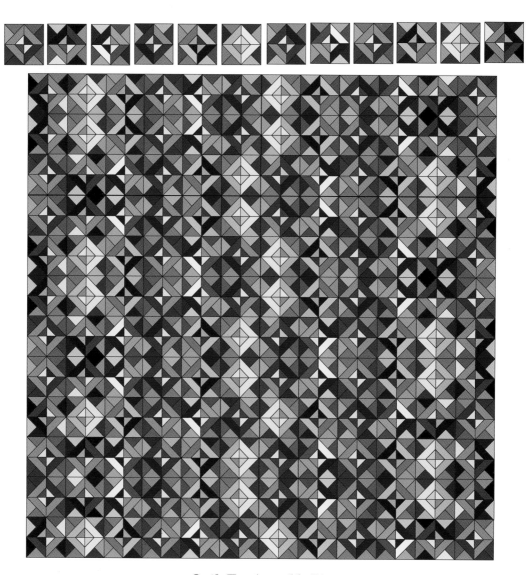

Quilt Top Assembly Diagram

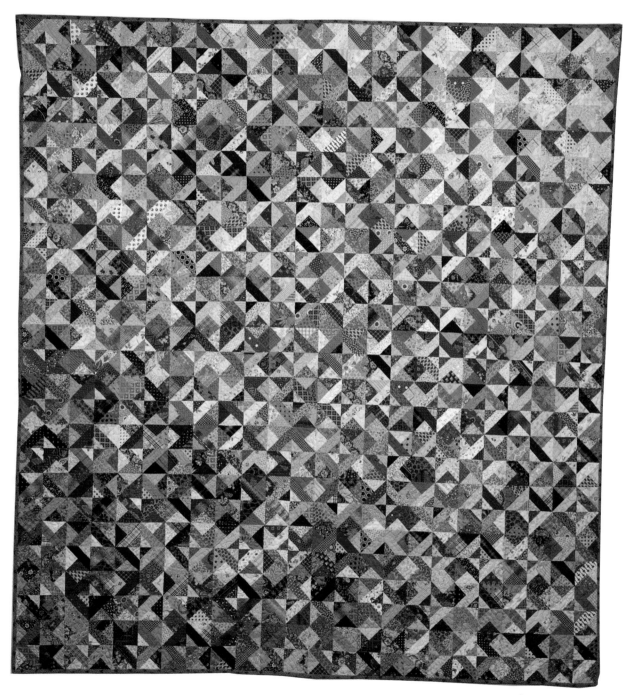

Little Bits Quilt
Designed and pieced by Edyta Sitar for Laundry Basket Quilts

Resources

Laundry Basket Quilts . . . . www.laundrybasketquilts.com

Moda Fabrics . . . . www.unitednotions.com

Aurifil™ Threads . . . . www.aurifil.com

Southern Exposure . . . . www.southernmoon.com

Quilting Creations International .www.quiltingcreations.com

Accomplish Quilting . . . . www.accomplishquilting.com

Hobbs Batting . . . . .www.hobbsbondedfibers.com

Bernina .www.berninausa.com

Creative Grids . . . . www.creativegridsusa.com

Long Arm Quilters—
Julie Lillo . . . . .www.quiltedjewels.com
Pam Henrys . . . . .www.everlasting stitches.com
Dan Kolbe .dckolbe@comcast.net

Landauer Corporation . . . . www.landauercorp.com